Praise for
For Women Only in the Workplace

"*The Male Factor* is full of practical recommendations for women who want to maximize their impact in a workplace full of male counterparts, and is a must-read for women in leadership. If you've ever interacted with a male colleague, boss, or employee, and wondered, "Why did he respond that way?" this book will provide the answers."

—Yvette Maher, vice president of Focus on the Family

"Shaunti Feldhahn has done it again! Revealing, insightful, but most of all unapologetically realistic, she shares in her latest offering, *For Women Only in the Workplace*, what women need to know in order to navigate through the workplace victoriously. The unwritten rules can no longer be ignored because Shaunti has spelled them out with crystal clarity. A must-read."

—Michelle McKinney Hammond, author of *What Women Don't Know and Men Don't Tell You*

"*For Women Only in the Workplace* is filled with practical research-based insights on how men view women in the workplace—insights you can use immediately to reach your professional goals faster and thrive in the workplace. If you find yourself confused by how your male boss or co-workers think or act, Shaunti Feldhahn peels back the layers to help you understand what's really going on. Candid and revealing, *For Women Only in the Workplace* is a wise read for professional women."

—Valorie Burton, author of *What's Really Holding You Back?* and *How Did I Get So Busy?*

Praise for
The Male Factor
(The general-market edition of *For Women Only in the Workplace*)

"*The Male Factor* is the singularly best business book for women I've read in years. This well-researched yet thoroughly readable book is rich with rare insights into how men really see women in the workplace—and how with a few simple adjustments you can even the playing field."

—LOIS P. FRANKEL, PhD, author of *Nice Girls Don't Get the Corner Office* and *See Jane Lead*

"Many times in my career I've been the only female in a meeting or holding a seat on the executive team, and I felt I needed a translator—either to understand my male colleagues or to make sure they understood me! *The Male Factor* provides that translation. We no longer have to guess at what makes men tick in the workplace. Shaunti Feldhahn asked them, and amazingly, they told her!"

—STACIE HAGAN, chief people officer at Earthlink Inc.

"Smart, effective communication is what makes for successful leadership and productive workplaces. *The Male Factor* sheds light on how subtle and not-so-subtle gender communication differences can thwart a woman's rise in the workplace. Even minor shifts in communication approach can help women navigate and break through that invisible barrier. There is something here for every woman, no matter where you are in your career."

—LINDA SAWYER, CEO of Deutsch Inc.

shaunti feldhahn

what you need to know about
how men think at work

for
women
only

in the
Workplace

MULTNOMAH
BOOKS

FOR WOMEN ONLY IN THE WORKPLACE
PUBLISHED BY MULTNOMAH BOOKS
12265 Oracle Boulevard, Suite 200
Colorado Springs, Colorado 80921

Scripture quotations and paraphrases are taken from the Holy Bible, New International Version®. NIV®. Copyright © 1973, 1978, 1984 by Biblica Inc.™. Used by permission of Zondervan. All rights reserved worldwide. www.zondervan.com.

ISBN 978-1-60142-378-8
ISBN 978-1-60142-395-5 (electronic)

Copyright © 2011 by Veritas Enterprises Inc.

Cover design by Mark Ford

Published in the United States by WaterBrook Multnomah, an imprint of the Crown Publishing Group, a division of Random House Inc., New York.

MULTNOMAH and its mountain colophon are registered trademarks of Random House Inc.

Previously published as *The Male Factor* by Multnomah Books and Crown Business in 2009.

Library of Congress Cataloging-in-Publication Data is on file with the Library of Congress.

Printed in the United States of America
2011—First Revised Edition

10 9 8 7 6 5 4 3 2 1

SPECIAL SALES
Most WaterBrook Multnomah books are available at special quantity discounts when purchased in bulk by corporations, organizations, and special-interest groups. Custom imprinting or excerpting can also be done to fit special needs. For information, please e-mail SpecialMarkets@ WaterBrookMultnomah.com or call 1-800-603-7051.

To Calvin and Nerida Edwards,
for twelve years of life-changing
collaboration and friendship

Contents

For Women Only in the Workplace
Research Team

Front, from left to right: Jenny Reynolds, research analyst; Shaunti Feldhahn, author; Linda Crews, director of operations; Karen Newby, research assistant. Back, from left to right: Kim Rash, content advisor; Vance Hanifen, research assistant; Calvin Edwards, content advisor; Jeff Feldhahn, content advisor; Leslie Hattenbach, research assistant. Not pictured: Jackie Coleman, research assistant; Ann Browne, co-founder, Human Factor Resources.

Above, left, the Decision Analyst team, left to right: Ramiro Davila, senior research analyst; J. Scott Hanson, PhD, vice president, Client Services; Felicia Rogers, executive vice president, Client Services.

Above, right, the Analytic Focus team, left to right: Charles Cowan, managing partner; Mauricio Vidaurre-Vega, research assistant.

Men 101

"Are you saying women don't already know that?"

The businessman sitting next to me in first class looked at me in disbelief. I was flying home from speaking at a women's conference, and we were only a few minutes into the usual "what do you do?" airplane conversation. Then I shared something that apparently stunned him. I had explained that I was a financial analyst by training, had worked on Wall Street, and was now, unexpectedly, an author, researcher, and speaker on relationships.

"I spent several years interviewing and surveying a few thousand men," I explained. "My last book, *For Women Only*, identifies ways men think and feel that women tend not to know."

He folded his arms across his chest and chuckled. "Okay," he said, "hit me with one."

So I shared one of my findings about men: They need respect so much, and find inadequacy so painful, that they would give up feeling loved if they could just feel respected. When I confirmed that even the most astute women may not know that particular truth about men, his amusement turned to disbelief. "That explains something!" he said finally. "You see, I'm a corporate trainer and consultant. Fortune 100 corporations bring me in to help with leadership and strategy at the highest levels of the organization. And all too often I see skilled and talented women sabotage their careers because they treat the men they work with in a way that no man would treat another man." He looked at me with awakening interest. "But from what you're telling me, these women probably don't even realize that is what they are doing."

I already had out my notebook and pen. "Can you give me an example?"

"I'll give you an example of something that just happened a few hours ago." For the next few minutes, he told me his story (which I'll relay in a later chapter) and concluded, "I was so puzzled why this female executive would shoot herself in the foot like that! But perhaps she simply didn't understand how her actions would be perceived by her colleagues—colleagues who were mostly men."

WE DON'T KNOW WHAT WE DON'T KNOW

After eight years of researching how men think, I'm still surprised at how much we women don't know about men—and how much this knowledge gap is affecting us at work and at home. As Scottish psychiatrist R. D. Lang memorably put it, "The range of what we think and do is limited by what we fail to notice. And, because we fail to notice that we fail to notice, there is little we can do to change until we notice how our failing to notice shapes our thoughts and deeds."

That's why I wrote this book. I want to show you those unwritten, unspoken, but very real male expectations and perceptions (including misperceptions!) that affect us every day at work, but that we would never otherwise know. As the opening conversation reveals, even as smart, experienced women, we can find ourselves being tripped up by obstacles we don't know are there. Or perhaps we simply aren't as influential as we could be, or aren't experiencing the rewarding, positive relationships that all of us want in the workplace. Based on my nationwide surveys and interviews with thousands of men, I can tell you that those dynamics are far more common than most women realize.

Whether you put in long hours at a Fortune 500 corporation or are a part-time volunteer in a ministry environment, the eye-opening insights you're about to encounter have the potential to transform your approach to relationships on the job. Proverbs 24 says it is correct *knowledge* that fills the key places in our lives with "rare and beautiful treasures"—and I think you'll find a correct understanding of men significantly improving not only your workplace effectiveness and influence, but also your personal fulfillment.

HOW I GOT HERE

I first realized the need for this new understanding in 2001 when I was writing my novel *The Lights of Tenth Street*; trying to figure out what my main male character would be thinking so I could put thoughts in his head. Talking to male colleagues or friends, I would describe a given workplace or home-life scene in the book, and ask, "What would you be thinking if this was you in this situation?" I was often stunned at the vital importance of what the men shared—and that after years of marriage and years of work in the male-dominated Wall Street arena, I was hearing most of it for the first time.

I began a multiyear project to investigate and write about the vital surprises that we most need to know. The first book in the series, *For Women Only*, focused on the personal-relationship side of things—and hit a nerve, selling one million copies in twenty different languages. Other research-based books for men, teens, and parents followed. But during that time, I continued to investigate the workplace application of the inner lives of men, eventually interviewing and surveying more than three thousand men to get their candid impressions. I would strike up a conversation with the anonymous man next to me on the airplane or subway, or schedule interviews with high-level executives in whatever city I had a speaking engagement that week, guaranteeing anonymity in writing to ensure I heard their candid, unfiltered perceptions.

To quantify the results, over the years I also commissioned three nationally representative surveys of men of all ages, races, stages of life, and backgrounds—including one major survey specifically for the workplace—teaming up with the nationally respected companies Decision Analyst and Analytic Focus to ensure I got reliable data. Chuck Cowan, the founder and president of Analytic Focus, and the former chief of survey design at the U.S. Census Bureau, has been my primary survey-design consultant for all my books. He explains the workplace survey's methodology in an article you'll find at ForWomenOnlyWorkplace.com. This long-term research process involved not only me but an entire team of staff researchers and outside specialists.

The end result is this book, released in two editions that are similar in core content but different in title and audience. The primary, general-market edition is a large hardcover version titled *The Male Factor*. When I speak at companies like Coca-Cola or Earthlink, that is the version I bring. (Take a look at *The Male Factor*, or my main business-market website, www.TheMaleFactorBook.com.)

But this edition, titled *For Women Only in the Workplace*, speaks primarily to readers looking for a Christian perspective, whether working in a secular or faith-based environment. Bonus features in this edition include Discussion Questions for readers' groups and an extra chapter, "Putting It in Perspective," which provides practical insight from experienced Christian women who have navigated these issues for years. To achieve the unique perspective of this edition, and make space for the extra material, I edited, trimmed and rearranged some of *The Male Factor* content, judiciously edited some of the men's quotes for space, and moved one of the chapters (about big-picture observations from my research) to my website for this book, www.ForWomenOnlyWorkplace.com.

ON TOP OF IT—AND STILL MISSING IT

It is ironic that the modern workplace finally recognizes the great business value of different perspectives and is filled with motivated, talented women, yet still has difficulty advancing women into leadership in the same numbers as men. Despite all our success at developing networking and mentoring programs, creating flexible working arrangements, and eliminating old-school bias, the numbers at the top haven't changed much. Women make up about half of entry-level professionals in most industries, but a much smaller percentage at any significant leadership level. Why is that?

There are many factors, of course, but two reasons stand out. Sometimes, women's job choices are simply different from men's: statistically, women are more likely to prioritize family-friendly flexibility and accept the trade-off in pay or advancement. But there's another reason as well—and this is one we can address with great effect if we try. It is what I call "the male factor": the degree to which a woman's workplace trajectory and effectiveness are being impacted, without her realizing it, by the unspoken expectations shared by most men—especially men in leadership. Giving the woman the information she needs to fill in that knowledge gap can make an enormous difference. As one senior executive said,

> Women in business have seen some tremendous opportunities open up, but have also seen that it is still "a man's world" in many ways. What I mean by that, though, is different than you think. Historically, for better or for worse, men pretty much created what we mean by "the business world" today. And since men still tend to hold most of the top-level positions, their subconscious ideas about how things should work are still framing the debate. It would be extremely helpful for women to have those insights.

DIGGING INTO THE SURPRISES

So when they're promised anonymity, what do men reveal that women would never otherwise know? What do men at work—regardless of their personality, industry, seniority level, age, race, religious belief, or any other differing factor—commonly expect of themselves and those they work with that women might not also expect? How do women trip themselves up without ever realizing it? And most important, how can we make use of these newfound insights to become more influential, effective, successful, and fulfilled in our working life?

The pages ahead provide the results of nearly a decade of research, investigation, and analysis to answer those questions. My research illuminates the biblical reality that men and women simply are created differently, including in ways that affect you but men would never tell you. These differences are critical for you to understand for the best working relationships, not because men's ways are right, or because you should necessarily adapt to their expectations, but because these perceptions exist and affect you whether you know it or not.

In many ways, understanding these unwritten perceptions is similar to understanding a foreign culture. One Christian businessman in an international services firm provided a helpful analogy:

When you do business with the Japanese, they require it to be done in a certain way. So we have to accommodate that. It's the same thing doing business in other cultures. When you do things with them, you have to do it in a certain way to be really productive. *Especially* if your natural inclination is not built that way, you have to really be aware of it and be willing to work and learn what they expect—not just what you expect. That's the way it works with what you're doing [helping women understand men]. In my previous firm, several of us spearheaded an effort to help change the good ol' boy culture to be more welcoming to women. But it works both ways. Just as if you were doing business with another culture, I would urge anyone, when in doubt, to be flexible and willing to learn.

Having worked with Japanese businessmen myself for three years on Wall Street, I understood exactly what he was saying. Some of the perceptions and suggestions in the chapters ahead may not align with our natural predispositions or preferences. There almost certainly will be cases where we simply decide that adjustments in our behavior or approach aren't appropriate or necessary. But there may also be many cases where, without compromising ourselves, it is in our interest to be flexible and willing to learn.

> *"Just as if you were doing business with another culture, I would urge anyone, when in doubt, to be flexible and willing to learn."*

Since knowing these hidden but real ideas and expectations will make you far more effective, I would argue that understanding men is a career-critical skill set women can develop like any other. But I would also argue that women of faith are called to do more than look out for our careers. We're called to understand and live by the truth of how God created each of us, and to "look out not only for [our] own interests, but also for the interests of others." We're called, as Romans says, to "be transformed by the renewing of [our] mind."

To actually accomplish those goals, though, we must set aside everything we think we know about men and how they view women.

In today's culture, we see a lot of cynicism about men, but I was both surprised and heartened to find that much of it is unwarranted. Yes, I heard men say many challenging things along the way, but every day I also became aware of how many men (often the same men!) had genuine goodwill toward women as equal partners in the workplace.

In this regard, my research surfaced four unmistakable big-picture patterns I want you to know about before we start (you can see more about these in the expanded "Observations" chapter that you can find at www.ForWomenOnlyWorkplace.com).

The men wanted to help women advance— and saw this knowledge as key

With few exceptions, the men I interviewed seemed to have a sincere desire to help women advance, both because they cared personally and because they knew it would be better for their organization. Most men were surprisingly aware of the external hurdles women encounter in business, often citing dilemmas faced by wives, girlfriends, daughters, or female colleagues that are rarely encountered by men. A busy leader's willingness to carve out time for an interview usually seemed directly tied to that genuine goodwill toward women.

Each man seemed to feel that even if some external hurdles still existed, he could at least help women avoid the self-inflicted ones caused by misunderstandings or gaps in knowledge, since, statistically, men still were likely to be in control at one time or another of the path upward. One senior executive, whom I will call Geoff,* the worldwide chief marketing officer (CMO) of a Fortune 500 company, provided this fascinating if blunt input in an interview:

---

*All names have been changed.

Women have to tell themselves, *In business, it's still a man's world.* That's changing slowly and you shouldn't accept it, but you do have to accurately evaluate the landscape. The better the evaluation, the better the results. You have to conduct yourself accordingly and say, "I won't compromise, but I will understand the rules." The only way to change the company is to get higher up.

As you rise through the ranks, no one is incompetent—so advancement comes from all the other factors. It's not just talent, because everyone has that. Instead it's the boss valuing trust, people who fit with his own style, and loyalty. It's so hard to break into those teams. You can have talent, but you have to earn loyalty.

The most senior executive I interviewed, Warren, is the president of a well-known Fortune 50 corporation, where he worked with countless women in different departments as he rose through the ranks. When I asked if he had one piece of advice he would have wanted to share with female colleagues, he provided an invaluable perspective:

It is the same thing I used to tell everyone back in my years in sales, or in our international division: Know your audience. Know how your audience is going to perceive how you are saying this. Women innately know how another woman is going to perceive something. They don't innately know how a man is going to perceive something. It is no use saying, "They shouldn't perceive it that way," when they do. But once you learn your audience, then you can gear yourself to be responsive to that audience.

On my main national survey, two out of three men said there were indeed areas in which talented women tripped themselves up because they didn't understand how they were being perceived by men.

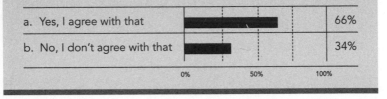

In your opinion, are there certain things that even skilled and talented women sometimes unintentionally do that undermine their effectiveness with men, simply because they don't realize how they are being perceived by the men they work with? Choose one answer.

a. Yes, I agree with that		66%
b. No, I don't agree with that		34%

0%   50%   100%

It was telling that the agreement was even higher (77 percent) among the critical bracket of men aged thirty-four to forty-four, who were more likely to be in the middle ranks of the organization, actually working with many female peers day to day, and competing with them for the path upward.

Even men of goodwill expressed uncomfortable perceptions at times

While I try to relay interview quotes only from men who I felt had a genuine desire to help women advance, I still found some of their comments to be challenging. In fact, my female research assistants and I sometimes found ourselves indignant when reviewing interview transcripts. Many times I fundamentally disagreed when a man who otherwise seemed very progressive made a sweeping generalization such as, "Women usually do such-and-such and men never do."

Thankfully, sweeping generalizations were few; it was much more common for men to be so cautious that it took me awhile to piece together the sometimes startling patterns in what they said. But for the purpose of understanding how men think, it really doesn't matter whether a man's perception is accurate and appropriately nuanced or not.

In recent decades, a great deal of effort has gone into improving perceptions of women in the workplace, and those efforts continue to be important. But I've come to realize they can also backfire if we don't pair them with a better understanding of why men have those impressions in the first place. Many of those perceptions stem from deep, foundational needs, fears, and truths common to many men. If we summarily dismiss an unpalatable remark or make certain discussions off-limits, we miss the opportunity to look past them to see if there is a deeper truth at work that women need to be aware of. We could end up hindering women's advancement instead of helping it. I heard a sobering number of examples where men "stuffed" annoyances with a particular female colleague rather than risk being misunderstood or labeled a chauvinist. But since other male co-workers privately felt the same way, the woman was eventually sidelined or frustrated in her working relationships—often without ever hearing the real issue or having the opportunity for self-improvement.

It does not demean women to go through the process of "knowing our audience," as Warren put it, and examining men's thoughts. Personally, I've seen over and again that it is in my best interest to identify and understand the impressions men have but don't feel they can say—especially so I can work to counter any thoughts that are inaccurate or unfair. The reverse is true as well; a parallel effort is needed for men in the workplace to better understand and correct common misperceptions about women.

Political correctness doesn't help

My male interviewees clearly felt a weight of concern about political correctness as we spoke. Probably three out of every four men were clearly trying hard to be judicious in their use of words, sometimes with long pauses while they sought for just the right phrasing to reassure me they were being as respectful as possible. (The other one out of four were often quite blunt and didn't seem to care what they said or what I might think about it. But they were also more likely to be strangers on an airplane than someone whose name and business I knew.)

It was encouraging that most men had clearly absorbed an internal desire to not even think, much less express, something perceived as disrespectful to women. Yet because of that, it required lots of trial and error to understand how to have a meaningful, honest interview, as well as much more effort to develop survey questions that men felt safe in answering.

Perceptions of Christian men were similar to all men in the workplace

I found few differences in how men thought based on any personal demographics (age, race, religious belief, etc.). As in my earlier surveys, men who described themselves as Christians sometimes described different *behavior* choices than their secular co-workers, but the personal, internal expectations and perceptions were usually much the same.

One male friend explained the phenomenon this way: "The renewing of our mind can change how a Christian thinks. But most of your findings relate to how God made men. Yes, most Christian men want to be better men, but we're still male in our impulses and perspectives."

OUR STARTING POINT

To get at the truth, my research was all about developing theories, testing them, and refining them to whatever degree I could. But I also wasn't starting from a blank slate, nor can I do so in this book. In the chapters ahead, to preserve my limited space for the key findings about men, I will be starting with several suppositions based on prior research and information:

- **Gender differences exist.** I don't pretend to know why men and women are created so different, or which differences result from nature or nurture. But nearly every relevant branch of science today recognizes that there are fundamental differences in the ways men's and women's brains are wired. I'll outline some of the clinical findings in the pages ahead, but for the most part I'll stick with focusing on how men think and feel in the workplace and let the men speak for themselves.

- **There are exceptions to every rule.** Despite the real differences between men and women, everyone is an individual. When I say that "most" men appear to share a particular perspective, I mean exactly that— most men, not all. Of necessity I will make some generalizations. One reason for the surveys was to understand what generalizations could be made, and what were the exceptions.

- **The differences are often in the details.** It is important to explicitly say that, despite our differences, women can identify with many things important to men. For example, just because I say that men value a "suck it up" mentality (chapter 5) or look for a particular type of professional respect (chapter 6), it does not mean that women don't. Quite often, the differences, and surprises, were in the details: the magnitude, frequency, or cause of a particular perception. For example, both men and women value respect, but it is surprising how unexpectedly easy it is for a man to feel that he's being *disrespected* by words or actions that a woman would never see that way. Similarly, I found that the highest-level women often shared viewpoints that were quite similar to men.

I also want to share a few caveats. Over the years, I've found how easy it is to be misunderstood on these subjects. So here, up front, are a few vital facts to keep in mind as you read the chapters ahead:

- **Explanation is not endorsement.** Some women mistakenly assume that identifying and explaining a commonly held male thought means that I endorse it. It's important for you to know I am not saying that men's assumptions are right (I've actually included quite a few that are wrong!), or that women must change to fit into a "man's world." This book can be used as much to help men examine their thoughts and assumptions as to help women understand them.

- **The real world has more balance.** Nearly every man gave me multiple examples where female colleagues were effective and "did it right," but for space reasons I couldn't balance every negative with a positive. In the pages ahead, I lean toward providing as many anti-self-sabotage principles as possible, even though this balance risks giving the impression that "all women do it wrong all the time," and that is not at all what the men were saying. Very much the reverse, in fact; they often went out of their way to point out cases where female colleagues were widely admired by men.

- **Women have strengths that men must understand as well.** It should go without saying, but I think it is important to say it anyway: God has gifted women with perspectives and strengths that are invaluable for the workplace—perspectives that men, on their side, may also misunderstand. Understanding men in those

situations doesn't mean compromising ourselves. We are
called to steward and nurture our gifts, and as one highly
respected Christian businessman pointed out, we are in
an era that provides "spectacular" opportunities for
women to do just that. It would be foolish for us to shut
down our strengths simply because they may be misunderstood by men. Instead, we may find that adjusting our
approach might be just what's needed for a mutual
understanding of one another's God-given differences.

> *I am not saying that men's assump-
> tions are right or that women must
> change to fit into a "man's world."*

BUCKLE YOUR SEAT BELTS

So you've heard my observations. Now get ready to make your own.
For there are sure to be surprising truths you read in these pages—
truths that you'll never hear from the men you work alongside
every day.

What you do with your observations will be important. Because
just as we are called to live in peace with one another by working
hard at personal relationships, we are called to have a similar attitude of willingness in the workplace, as though we were working for
the Lord rather than for people, as the apostle Paul put it.

Hopefully, in your work life you have already experienced one
of the main reasons why God asks us to think of it that way. When
we set aside our personal preferences or knee-jerk reactions and remember that we have given our lives over to His purposes, we'll find
ourselves in grander adventures than we ever could have imagined.
And, despite the inevitable challenges, we'll be far more effective,
successful, and content in the end.

CHAPTER 1

"It's Not Personal; It's Business"

Welcome to Two Different Worlds

One theme running through the romantic comedy *You've Got Mail* is just how differently men and women view the concept "It's not personal; it's business." In the movie, Joe Fox (played by Tom Hanks) owns a massive Barnes & Noble–like bookstore chain that opens an outlet near a beloved children's bookshop run by Kathleen Kelly (Meg Ryan). Kathleen is unable to match their discount prices and tries valiantly to hang on, but eventually goes out of business. Joe discovers that the woman he's been ruthlessly competing with in business is also the anonymous woman he's fallen in love with online, the woman to whom he had given business advice such as, "Fight to the death" and "You're at war. It's not personal; it's business."

Later, he starts to apologize for putting her out of business, saying, "It wasn't personal—"

Kathleen interrupts: "What is that supposed to mean? I'm so sick of that. All that means is that it wasn't personal to *you.* But it was personal to me. It's personal to a lot of people. What is so wrong with being personal anyway?"

That short exchange captures a common source of friction I heard many times as I interviewed men and women about how each views their working life.

Many women tend to have a holistic view of the world, one where personal, family, and work matters are all viewed as part of the big picture called life.

As a result, women tend to have the same feelings and perspectives in different areas of their lives. When we are feeling attacked, underappreciated, or disappointed at work, and someone says, "It's not personal," that doesn't ring true to us. *Well, it's sure personal to me.*

Men, on the other hand, tend to have a very different view. It is as if they exist in two different worlds: Work World and Personal World. For a man, the two are utterly distinct and function by different rules: it is as if they are governed by different natural laws. So every morning when a man heads to work, he feels as if he physically leaves behind one world with one set of innate rules, crosses an emotional bridge, and enters a totally different world with a different set of rules and expectations. This experience tends to be as true for men in a ministry as men in the marketplace.

To women, the compartmentalization that results can come across as impersonal or lacking in compassion. Yet many of the godly men I spoke to said they could care about others and still feel work is a very different world.

> *In a man's mind, it is as if there are two different worlds: Work World and Personal World.*

Richard, president of a financial advisory group working with many ministries, captures that male experience:

> Business becomes its own box. The man presses the button for the tenth floor, and when he walks off the elevator, he's now in Business. Everything about the rest of the world gets suspended. It's not personal, not relational, not religious, not civic: it's business. When he says,

"It's not personal; it's business," he means that. It's like, "Don't you get it? I've crossed the bridge to the business world, and until I cross the bridge back home, this is where I am. There are rules here, written and unwritten, that govern this world." The idea of the business world is a construct men have learned to embrace. It may be a fiction of their mind, but to them it's very real.

The graphic below is an attempt to capture this difference visually:

TWO DIFFERENT WAYS OF VIEWING THE WORLD:

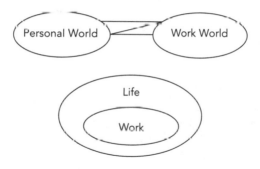

Because of these two very different ways of looking at the world, a phrase like "It's not personal; it's business" tends to mean something different to men than women realize—or than we mean when we say the same thing. For instance, women might use that phrase to mean, "I know this situation [layoff or missed promotion] is personally difficult, but please realize this is not about you. I care about you personally, but this decision had to be made for purely business reasons." Men, on the other hand, usually mean, "You and I are not in Personal World now. We are in Work World. So we are handling this by the rules of Work World, and that is how you should perceive it. You shouldn't even have the same feelings as in Personal World."

While this rigid distinction loosens somewhat in ministries and faith-influenced settings, it never goes away entirely. On my survey, six in ten men said the working world simply functions by different rules. I was surprised the number wasn't higher, given men's overwhelming agreement with the question in my interviews, so I cross-tabbed this theoretical question with several that provided workplace examples. I discovered that once men were confronted with real-life scenarios, every single man did expect the working world to operate differently from the personal world.[1]

Stop and think for a moment about your view of working life and personal life. Which statement best describes your view?*
(Choose one answer.)

a. Things operate differently at work than they do in your personal life. You can adhere to the same values or personality in each place (for example, being honest, or compassionate), but the expectations and culture of each are simply different, so you adjust to each.

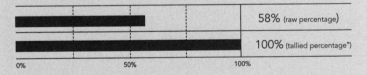

b. The way work life and personal life operate are not that different, so you can operate pretty much the same in both arenas.

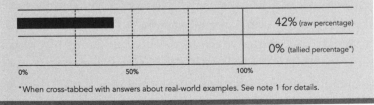

*When cross-tabbed with answers about real-world examples. See note 1 for details.

The men were clear that it is the operating rules of the environment that change, not a person's personality or values. In their minds, they are the same individual with the same temperament and values in each world. But the environment has changed around them, and so they adapt to the rules governing that environment.

A good analogy would be as if in one world they are playing the game of paintball, while in the other world they play poker. The player is the same person, with the same values—for example, "one should never cheat"—but (in the man's mind) it is as if there really are two completely different games with completely different rules.

For us to be most effective—and, frankly, to be able to catch any incorrect perceptions of us—we need to know what our male colleagues, employees, bosses, and customers see as "the rules" of Work World, and just how deeply those expectations are embedded in the male psyche.

As noted, I am not suggesting that a man's expectations and perceptions are right or wrong, or that women necessarily need to change the way they work to adapt to them. But it is in our best interest to understand what they are. I also think it's important to understand the inner wiring in a man that leads to those expectations in the first place.

A MAN'S INNER WIRING

Men's beliefs at work seem to arise from three facts about how their brains have been created, and how they have related to other males since childhood.

1. The male brain naturally compartmentalizes

The male brain tends to find mental multitasking difficult and is set up to naturally compartmentalize emotions, thoughts, and sensory inputs—whereas the female brain is the other way around. That is a simple summary of a complex truth.

In our book *For Men Only*, my husband and I compared a woman's thought life to a personal computer with multiple windows open at a time. Most women know what it's like to be aware of, thinking about, or actually doing many things at once, and can transition seamlessly back and forth between personal and work tasks. I love the example of the Proverbs 31 woman, who is running a business, caring for her home, managing her servants, making clothes, and helping the poor—seemingly all at once!

Neuroscientists have discovered that anyone's ability to multi-task like this depends in large part on the amount and type of connectivity along the corpus callosum, the main superhighway between the left and right hemispheres of the brain. A 1999 *Journal of Neuroscience* study demonstrated that the influence of estrogen gives women far more of that connectivity, and thus a great ability and predisposition to think about and do many things at once.[2] The downside to being able to manage all those open windows simultaneously, however, is that most women (81 percent according to our survey) have a hard time closing down thoughts that nag them.

Most men, by contrast, find it exhausting just to think about all those multiple windows. A man's thought life is more like a computer with one window open at a time. He works on it, closes it, then opens another, and usually has no trouble closing out thoughts that bother him.

You may have noticed that tendency for a man to tell his wife, "Just don't think about it." That advice may seem easy to him but feels impossible for her, and there is a biological reason for it: he is far more predisposed to compartmentalize, and better at it. Brain scientists have discovered that a person's tendency to compartmentalize stems from fewer connections within their corpus callosum superhighway, as well as its unique makeup. According to researcher Rita Carter and neuropsychologist Christopher Frith in *Mapping the Mind*, the corpus callosum is 25 percent smaller in men than in women.[3] Further, a team of Israeli fetal researchers found that the in-utero influence of testosterone decreases the growth of nerve connections between the hemispheres, making mental multitasking much more difficult for men.[4]

But what men gain from their brain structure is a superior ability to compartmentalize and deeply process various functions and thoughts without being distracted.

Add to this what neuropsychiatrists at the University of Pennsylvania found: Within the corpus callosum, men have far more gray matter (where thinking and functioning occur) than women, who have far more of the connecting white matter used to send those thoughts from one area of gray matter to the next. As a result, men's thoughts are more isolated, less interconnected, and more compartmentalized. As Dr. Raquel E. Gur explained in the 1999 study, this promotes men's extreme ability to concentrate within any one mode of thinking or functioning without being distracted by a connection to another type of thought.[5]

In other words, men's tendency to segregate "personal" from "work" is something they do automatically without thinking about it—both because their brains are structured for it, and because their brains aren't structured to bounce thoughts back and forth between worlds easily. And as you'll see, that affects almost everything about how men think, feel, and process information.

> Men's tendency to segregate personal and work is something they do automatically without thinking about it, in part due to their brain structure.

Many women have noticed one direct outcome of this. Unlike women, once men cross the bridge into Work World, it is as if Personal World vanishes into the mist during the workday. One Christian businessman I know is a very empathetic guy, yet as he put it, "While I'm sitting here at work, I have to almost go into a different world in my mind even to tell you my daughters' names."

Another direct outcome of this compartmentalized brain wiring is a man's tendency to separate himself and his personal feelings from the job. One executive brought up a perfect illustration of this by drawing upon an old Looney Tunes short cartoon. In the cartoon, Ralph Wolf and Sam Sheepdog walk to work, chatting personably ("Morning, Ralph!" "Morning, Sam!"), clock in, and take up their positions. When the work whistle blows, Ralph and Sam clash and fight each other intensely. Ralph's job is to try to steal and eat the sheep, and Sam's is to protect them. They try to blow each other up and bash each other on the head until the lunch whistle blows. Then they stop in midbash, go companionably to share a meal, and after stretching and yawning, return to their positions with Sam's hand clenched around Ralph's throat. The executive I spoke with said this is precisely how men view life: they completely distinguish between personal and business, and one has little or no effect on the other. One man in the broadcasting industry gave me a real-world version of Ralph and Sam—a story I've heard, in essence, from many other men:

> I used to work with a guy, Bob, at Network A. When one of the key players who had worked with Bob and was his good friend moved on to the CEO position at Network B, he brought along Bob to see if he could take a crack at transitioning to a new type of sales. A year later, this guy fired Bob because he wasn't measuring up to expectations. Bob wasn't selling enough…he just couldn't make the transition. Now, the thing is: Bob and the CEO continue to be the closest friends. They go on vacations together. I just saw Bob recently, and he and his wife had just come back from a visit to the CEO's beach house in Florida.

I met this executive at a restaurant with his wife. She owns a thriving retail store herself and told me, "I've had to fire people several times and been fired myself. I can't imagine still wanting to be close friends afterward. I don't know how he does it."

Her husband shrugged. "A lot of this has to do with an ability to compartmentalize, and that comes with experience. When you get higher up, you understand the mentality and understand the whole business process. When Carly Fiorina was fired from Hewlett-Packard, I don't think it was because the board didn't like her, and I'm sure she didn't take it personally. The more experienced you are, the more you compartmentalize."

In other words, this executive assumed that the more experienced you were in business, the more you would compartmentalize, and that the less you did so, the less businesslike you were. As I listened, I couldn't help but think, *I wonder what he would say if I told him compartmentalization has more to do with brain structure than with experience?*

2. The male brain becomes ultrafocused

A man's brain structure and hormone mix also give him a greater ability to become hyperfocused on whatever project is at hand. A few ramifications:

Everything else gets screened out—and that feels great. Most men I spoke with described the ability to go into this focused state as important for their productivity (which makes sense, given their relative difficulty with multitasking). Everything else gets screened out, and men describe going into that intense zone as providing the same sort of high as a postexercise endorphin rush.

The downside, though, is that a man can also miss or screen out things that shouldn't be overlooked. It may be an actual decision to screen out something the man thinks of as "personal feelings" or "extraneous," or it may be that he's so focused on Project A that he's missing the impact of that on Project B (or on Person B).

The chief financial officer of a Fortune 500 manufacturer explained, "Men tend to look back and say, 'Oh shoot, there were victims along the way.' We can be oblivious to all the other things going on, but it's not a lack of care. Not at all. You're trained as a kid that winning is everything. Your competitive juices flow and you hurt the other guy, or yourself, and you don't even notice." That sort of miss-every-thing-else focus is not at all unusual for men. At times, what may look like male insensitivity or even callousness may actually be a simple function of brain anatomy.

Anything that interrupts a man's natural focus is dispropor-tionately disruptive. While being intensely focused feels great to a man and allows him to be productive, not being able to focus in-tensely on one thing feels not just unproductive, but disconcerting and incredibly frustrating. This was apparent when I showed two software executives, David and Gregg, the Personal/Work World graphic on page 19.

DAVID: I love my wife and daughter, but if either of them calls me during the day, it is a real distraction. I have to expend extra effort to get back into work mode, extra effort I wouldn't other-wise have to spend. Men have limited capacity to deal with uninvited distractions, and I just lost some of my capacity right there.

GREGG: It's not that with this intrusion you've lost the connection to the work world. That's not it at all.

DAVID: It's that there's this other thought open in your mind that prevents you from being 100 percent efficient.

GREGG: Yesterday morning was a good example. My wife asked if I could run by the house over lunch and drop the dog at the vet.

She didn't think it was a big deal. It is over lunch, after all. But until that's resolved—"I got the dog and I'm back"—somewhere out there I know I'm going to have to take an hour and go get the dog. Just having that open thought in the back of my mind is disruptive.

3. Men strive to protect themselves from emotional pain

Men are far more sensitive to being hurt than most women realize. In many ways, a man's compartmentalizing of emotions and creating a tough facade exists to cover a vulnerable interior that he feels a strong need to protect—especially since most men don't feel as natural or adept at handling their emotions as women.

One man I know, Eddie, had a tough time emotionally when his consulting contract with a good friend from church was terminated unexpectedly. He was a complete contrast to the story I told earlier about the broadcast salesman who continued to vacation with the boss who had fired him. A mutual friend explained,

> Eddie really pours himself into things. He puts his heart out there. That is why most other guys set up this idea of these two different worlds, business and personal. What wounded Eddie was his level of expectation. His boss was a close friend before and during the whole contract. I'm guessing Eddie allowed himself to feel like it wasn't just business, it was personal. And that's when it hurts. If Eddie had been just an arm's-length consultant, he would have said, "It's business," and moved on.
>
> From a guy's perspective, it is totally self-protective to have these "it's business" rules, because once you make it personal, it hurts so much. Guys know we don't do personal things as well as we want. We know that with our

families, when personal issues come up, it's complex and confusing, so business is almost a sanctuary or oasis away from those jumbled emotions. When we let the two worlds intersect, we not only impact the efficiency of the business but our ability to do it well and survive emotionally.

Doesn't your perspective change when you realize men didn't formulate or subscribe to the "it's not personal" rules of Work World because they have no emotion? Men created the rules because emotion is often so hard for them to handle. No wonder that even in faith-based ventures that often place a higher value on nurture, men still tend to maintain separate work and personal expectations.

> "From a guy's perspective, it is totally self-protective to have these 'it's business' rules, because once you make it personal, it hurts."

THE UNWRITTEN RULES OF WORK WORLD

So what are those expectations? How do men think Work World functions? First, remember, these aren't "tried and true tips for how business works best." Men view these as the "natural laws" that are just as inescapable in business as the law of gravity is in the physical world. (And although I am focusing on the expectations instinctively shared by most men, experienced female readers may see that they share some of them as well.)

Each rule is based on one overriding principle: everything happening at work must advance the goals of the organization and one's role within it as effectively as possible.

Now let's take a look at just four of the "unwritten rules" I heard most often (there are others, but many of them are covered in the chapters ahead).

1. You can't take things personally

In men's minds, you can take things personally in Personal World, but in Work World, whatever is going on is not about you—it's about the business. My core question in all my interviews and surveys was, essentially, "Is there anything that you've seen talented women do that undermines their effectiveness with men, simply because the women don't realize how it is being perceived?" One of the most common things I heard was, "Women sometimes take things too personally."

The CEO and COO of a well-known $5.5 billion organization, leading thousands of employees, had a unique perspective on this. For years, the organization had no well-defined performance measures or employee-evaluation system. Marty, the CEO, had brought in a new chief operating officer to change that. The COO, Ronald, had come from another household-name company with an excellent system of performance measurement and review, and had spent the previous year applying it to the new environment. I interviewed Marty and Ronald together. When I asked them if there was anything women might do that undermines their effectiveness, they glanced at each other with raised eyebrows.

MARTY: It's probably most apparent to me in performance reviews. This has been a real struggle for us, because we're trying to be nice, but we are putting some pretty strict performance metrics in place to measure what we do. It enables me to do a performance evaluation and quantify why I'm rating someone a certain way.

RONALD: The men have been a piece of cake, but we struggled with the women. When we tell employees they need to improve, the men just hear, "You did not do what we needed. What will you do to get better?" When we work with the women, we can have the same data in front of us, but they seem to hear, *We do not like you.*

MARTY: The men may say, "Well, I disagree with you about that." Or, "That's fine." Then it's over. It's not that way with the women, even the senior women.

Behind the scenes, I heard many examples of what "taking it personally" looked like to a man. Here's one example.

FROM THE OWNER OF AN ADVERTISING COMPANY

This week, I told one of my midlevel staff that she had to speed up. A lot of our deadlines are like dominoes, with everyone depending on everyone else meeting deadlines so all the moving parts mesh. Our staff members know they are measured by three things: how well they do on client visits, on the content of their projects, and turning things in on time. She was doing two of these three really well for how experienced she was.

I had to tell her that one of the three was below standard and we'd missed a client deadline because of her; and that client had specifically told us their deadlines were not negotiable. So when I spoke to her, I told her we had a single problem: You have to speed up.

But I could just tell that she was not hearing, "You need to speed up." She was hearing, "You've failed, you've let me down, this isn't working, I'm disappointed in you." I'd said: "You need to speed up."

Now, I could see this happening, and so I had to circle back around to tell her, "I need to be sure you know I'm only saying this one thing." But I could tell she was wounded, and I couldn't get her to focus and hear what I was saying. The moment she took it all personally, the meeting went out the window. I was trying to move to ongoing strategy, and I never got there. I was *trying* to get to the next step of saying, "Here are some ideas on speeding up," but I never got there because in my view she took the whole thing personally.

She apparently cried after I left the room. And I had to tell the other partners, "I met with her, but she wasn't able to hear what I was saying, and I don't think it's going to make any real difference."

Of course, you might be wondering, *But how can you not take things personally?* I put that question to a banking executive, Niles, who had just had to fire a key female manager the day before I spoke with him. "Because it is about your work, not about who you are," he answered. "It is not that I dislike you—you may be a wonderful person, have a great sense of humor, and be great to work with. But you have to recognize that the assignments you were given were not up to the standards set."

Having spent years hearing how much a man's identity is tied up in what he does and in his ability to provide for his family, I said I would have expected men to take it *more* personally if they were fired. Niles responded,

There is an element of taking it personally even for men. A little bit, because you are what your work is. But I have been fired, and I would then tell myself, *Well, I may not have given it my best effort,* or, *I was a square peg in a round hole and wasn't able to deliver up to expectations.* After all, if I was hired by NASA to launch a rocket, regardless of how hard I tried, I wouldn't be able to do it. I didn't have the skill set or experience. There are any number of reasons why someone might receive a poor evaluation. For whatever reason, that person may be in over their head. As long as his boss doesn't get personal, critical, and mean, a man might go home and get upset when he talks to his wife, but he won't take it personally at work.

Niles's comment points out a common (and eye-opening) distinction: in a man's mind, you can be quite *upset* about the situation itself and *yet still not take it personally.*

That said, despite the men's overwhelming unanimity on this point, I believe men's assurance that they never take things personally sounds better in theory than it sometimes works in practice. As I'll describe in a later chapter, I have found that there are certain things men are more likely to take personally than women. Yet that doesn't negate the primary point that they expect people in the workplace to take nothing personally and look askance at those who do.

2. You become your position

Another unwritten rule is that a job holder is essentially seen as a temporary holder and custodian of his or her position—a position that, in most cases, exists independent of the person and will be there after they leave. The implications of this perception are that, as cold as it sounds, the function of the position is more mission critical to the organization than the person doing it, and the position holder is supposed to do what is best for the company rather than for the individual.

Most organizational leaders understand that their greatest strength is their people and the passion and talent they bring to their work. Yet the fact remains that when group ABC needs a fundraising director or a programmer in the IT department, the group is trying to find the best person to fit a particular position or role, and that that position usually does exist independent of the person. As a result, when you walk through the company doors, you are, essentially, seen as a particular role as much as an individual.

One man I interviewed, whom I'll call Cole, is the founder and owner of a well-respected executive search firm that places C-level executives with Fortune 500 companies. He makes this distinction between himself and his job:

> I have fired a lot of people over the years. I'm a very empa-
> thetic person, and firing is always emotionally disconcerting
> to me, but it's one of the things I have to do. I often picture
> myself sitting in another chair as a third party, directing a
> play. It is not Cole firing Shaunti. It is the president firing a
> vice president. It is the director firing a manager. If you've
> got a role, you've got to play the role, like a doctor has to
> remove a tumor or a dentist has to pull a tooth. They've got
> bad jobs today. My job today is a bad job. I have to termi-
> nate somebody and I am not going to enjoy it. But that is
> my job. So when I say it is "just business," it does not mean I
> do not care about you. The dentist undoubtedly cares about
> the person whose tooth is failing. The doctor cares about
> the person whose tumor needs to be removed. But they do
> not let their concern for that person overshadow their
> responsibility. If you are failing in your role, my job is to
> confront you in a way that either beneficially resolves your
> failure to perform, or removes you so your failure does not
> create a broad-spread failure of the organization.

The ability men have to see themselves as separate from their business role is another key reason why they are able to take things less personally at work. Their personal identity is still tied to their job, but they can choose to see challenges or criticism as more about their position and less about them.

> "So when I say it is 'just business,' it does not mean I do not care about you. A worker cannot let his concern for a person overshadow his responsibility."

Of course, there are times when a person's expectations and those for his or her position collide. Then the expectation of the working world is for employees to fill the role to the best of their ability, rather than do what they personally prefer or even think best. In other words, if you have to choose, you subordinate your preferences to your position—and boss.

Here's an example from my own experience. At the Federal Reserve Bank of New York, my job involved detailed analysis into the facts—as far as I needed to go to get the truth. Working with Japanese banks that (like many international institutions) didn't have the same standards for disclosure often put me in the position of being a kind of financial detective, trying to uncover and fit together facts that others would prefer to stay hidden. I often had short deadlines and would work around the clock to do as much analysis as I felt was needed to understand what was going on and properly brief senior officials.

Later, however, when I moved to Atlanta and began working as an independent analyst for a consulting company, I found myself clashing with my employer. I was doing the same sort of work but now was billing hours on projects that would earn my employer a fixed fee. My boss kept asking me to cut down my hours for a certain type of report. I responded, "If I'm going to do it right, it will take at least twenty-five hours to do this type of analysis."

Finally he said, "You're not hearing me. I've bid a certain amount for this project. That is what the client will pay me, no matter how much time you take. If you keep billing me twenty-five hours for these reports, I'm going to lose money employing you. You may think what you're doing can't be done in under twenty-five hours, but I'm asking you to do a different type of analysis: the seventeen-hour version."

That's an example of how what I thought best as an experienced specialist clashed with my position, which was, when it came right down to it, to make money for the company, not lose it.

In my interviews with men, I heard dozens of examples of men becoming exasperated with an employee—almost always a female employee—who wouldn't stop arguing over something she found important. Men were puzzled and frustrated as to why these employees couldn't simply register their opinion and analysis about why something should be otherwise, then accept and faithfully implement their boss's decision, even if it differed from their preferences. Kevin, a national human resources director for a major consulting firm, said, "Men have these issues and concerns too, obviously, but they tend to be able to overlook them when they need to. Women tend to have more difficulty looking past small issues. If their point of view is not the one that the team decides to pursue, they may have a harder time accepting that and moving on. They tend to let smaller issues bother them and get in the way of accomplishing the bigger goal."

Now, what Kevin sees as a difficulty in looking past small issues may actually be the relative inability to close those mental "windows" that are bothering her—and the reason they are bothering her is often because she sees an unresolved issue that could come back to haunt the group or company. When I asked men how a woman should handle such a situation, by far the most common answer was probably not what we want to hear.

One man representatively suggested, "Document concerns in a short, clear e-mail to be sure you've been heard correctly. Then you need to explicitly say, 'but you're the boss,' and let it go. He has heard you, considered your point of view, and made a different judgment call. You may disagree with it, but it is his call to make, and you'll only hurt yourself by implying he's being stupid."

3. You don't make business decisions based on personal factors

One rule that men feel governs business isn't always perfectly followed by either gender: when you are at work, you do not make decisions based on factors considered personal, such as how you feel about someone, circumstances outside Work World, or your emotional response to a particular person or situation. Jackson, who ran a start-up company, described the premise this way:

> When I'm in business mode, I'm not operating out of the emotional sensibilities that I would be operating from in my personal life. I may be ticked off at you, but I can separate that for the good of the enterprise. Or I may think you're the best person around, but I can't let that feeling, which belongs on the personal side, dictate what I deem best for business. In personal life, personal feelings matter. In business life, personal feelings shouldn't be a consideration, except to the degree that they affect business. My employees are very loyal, and people seem to like working for me, so I hope I'm not an ogre. Still, I've got a family to provide for, so I'm not here to win a

popularity contest. If anyone's feelings are going to get hurt, it's not going to be my wife's because we're on food stamps. Now if being liked helps my job, I'm all for it. Otherwise, if by trying to be everyone's best friend it hurts my job or my business, that's gotta change.

> "In business life, personal feelings shouldn't be a consideration, except to the degree that they affect business."

Now, I've viewed some men as breaking this rule. I've experienced the good ol' boy network at work, been frustrated by being left out of ostensibly personal outings where work was discussed, and known of business contracts awarded and decisions based on what looked like outside personal relationships.

To help me understand this apparent contradiction (and others), I set up a day-long focus group of six experienced businessmen and two high-level women. All the men were unanimous in insisting that what I perceived as inconsistencies in men's actions and behavior weren't so at all. There are times, they said, when factors that seem personal are in fact best for the business.

For example, if a man gives a subcontract to a golf buddy instead of conducting an open bid, it is because the easy option of employing someone he knows and trusts allows more time and resources to be spent on more critical priorities. As one man put it, "'Not making decisions based on personal factors' doesn't mean 'you always do a systematic study of every conceivable option to choose the best one.'" Men agreed that if anyone did allow a personal factor to trump a business purpose, they would definitely be viewed as nonbusinesslike and as breaking a core business expectation.

Similarly, I was confused by a seeming contradiction on the

positive side. Many men I interviewed talked about the importance of considering employee feelings and morale, which seemed, to me, to be what men would otherwise describe as Personal World behavior. In one case, I heard about a Christian business owner who had recently treated a key employee kindly when her son was sick, even though she missed a critical deadline. He explained why it wasn't "personal":

> What I did was a strategy of sound business. I do care about her as a person, but my interest at work is that she's valuable and I need to keep her happy, motivated, and productive so our shared goals can be achieved. The guy who screams at her has similarly made a business decision. In my opinion, he has a flawed strategy that is likely to be counterproductive. But neither approach is personal. It's all about business, executed with different strategies.
>
> If I treated someone unkindly, it would be because I was having a bad day, not because it was a business decision. And then it *would* be personal, it *would* be operating according to rules of the personal world, where you let your emotions get the better of you. It would be wrong and regrettable, not just because it goes against a value of treating people well, but because it is letting personal circumstances impact what is best for business.

4. Emotions in the workplace have to be related to the business

Men brought up the subject of emotions in nearly every interview. It is so central that I've devoted the entire next chapter to it. In men's perceived rules of the workplace, it is expected that people show certain emotions only when they are related to the business (and then only infrequently). One man I met, Douglass, is a great Christian guy who is also in charge of an internationally known corporate-sponsorship group. Even though he seemed to be an exception in not minding certain emotions, he commented about what emotions will always be viewed as inappropriate at work:

> Even in a tough environment, I have seen women tear up and even some cry, and it has been totally fine because it has been appropriate. If anything, in a right setting it can cause a man to think, *Oh man, what have I done?* and wake up to the fact he's not handling something right. One time we had to fire a woman here, and when we told her, she teared up and had a rough time with it, but that was totally appropriate. She's losing her job. I don't expect her to be a robot. When it is not appropriate, ever, is when a woman cries in the workplace over something that does not have anything do with what is going on, like when a deal is falling apart and it has nothing to do with us. Honestly, some women tend to take things personally that should not be taken personally.

Similarly, because people are filling a position that is separate from them personally, men think that even intense conflicts should never carry over beyond the issue at hand. Think Ralph Wolf and Sam Sheepdog. A majority of men I spoke with brought up this issue as something they perceived women handling very differently from men. One finance manager pointed to my diagram about Personal World and Work World and said something I've heard dozens of times: "I've been in meetings where I had heated disagreements with guys, and later that day, we're having a beer and talking about the game. Men went back to the personal side of the bridge. If a woman was heated, it would be much more difficult to go bowling later."

THE PERSONAL COST OF
GETTING IT WRONG

Now it's time to ask the obvious but fairly daunting question: what happens when someone brings Personal World rules to Work World?

In my interviews, it seemed as if men mentally placed everyone they worked with in one of two camps: those who remember which world they are in and operate accordingly, and those who don't appear to remember they are in Work World and operate as if in Personal World. If the men saw someone operating within the rules of Work World, they viewed that person more positively. Colleagues, regardless of gender, appearing to operate by practices that belonged in Personal World were viewed more negatively.

Most men I surveyed felt that they rarely mixed up their worlds, where women did so regularly. (Not that most women did so, but that most of those who did so were women.) It is worth noting that the rare man who was seen as taking things personally or getting emotional at work was viewed much more harshly than a woman doing the same thing; he was viewed as a bit "off."

So what do men think when they see a colleague operating by Personal World rules? The men tended to have one or more of the following perceptions, most of which, clearly, are misperceptions:

- **"This person lacks self-confidence and self-esteem."**
  Look at this telling quote from Norm, a finance executive:

  "It's not just women who take things too personally. I have seen it in men every now and then too, and it sabotages their careers. It shows they lack self-confidence and self-esteem. Women who are successful have self-confidence enough to say, 'This isn't about me; it's about the task we have to perform.' They realize it's actually about the other person and that person's perception: 'So Bob didn't like this particular proposal. Well, a hundred other people might like it, but Bob is the boss, so I accept it and move on.'"

- **"This person is emotional, insecure, and lacks self-control."** Men frequently associated those who took things personally and broke other Work World rules as being emotional. This has a host of negative repercussions discussed more in the next chapter. It also seemed insecure and defensive. As one man said, "It looks like this constant, 'I've got something to prove. I've got to show you I'm in charge' thing. It makes them look like it's not about taking actions to get their work done, but more about showing 'I've got the power!'"

- **"This person is not a team player."** Over and again, I heard men carefully suggest that women sometimes did not come across as team players. This puzzled me since, empirically, women tend to be more collaborative than independent. Finally, I realized the perception came from something as innocuous as not taking your personal self out of it. Norm, the finance executive quoted earlier, used a military analogy: "If you can get with the mission and take the hill and convince people to follow you, you'll be successful. But to do that, you have to take your whole personal self out of it. That is what boot camp does. Like the military, business needs to be a team sport to succeed."

- **"This person is not mature, sophisticated, or business savvy."** Someone who doesn't adhere to the perceived natural laws of the working world isn't seen as business-like. For example, one senior partner at a worldwide accounting and consulting firm cited an example about gossiping. Among men, he said, there's an unwritten rule: if a man passes on unsubstantiated information, he says, "I don't know if this is true, but you might want to look at it." More likely, he says, "The man would go to the source and deal with something directly, while some women will talk around the office. It is not very business savvy to do that. It is human nature to think, *If I've got goodies, I want to share them,* but it is a sign of maturity when you don't have to share."

Not surprisingly, perceptions of an employee as more emotional, less secure, and naive could undermine or sidetrack a person's effectiveness or career. Geoff, the Fortune 500 CMO, observed,

A woman who doesn't understand how men think won't necessarily get herself into a fix, but she'll get herself into the neutral zone, and that's not a good place to be. She won't get into the club. If you're thought to be high maintenance, if your behavior is not predictable, if someone's not sure where you'll come out or thinks you could cause a fuss, if you don't get the silent code, if you're not a team player—it all gets you into the neutral zone. You will not be sought out or you'll be marginalized, even if you're smart. This happens to women much more than men, simply because men tend to instinctively understand what they did that caused that perception and either self-correct or know they have to get out. A woman may still get good reviews—neutral or positive. She reads this as mixed signals. A guy wouldn't. He would know he has to move.

I asked Geoff what women should look for, what danger signals should be heeded. He said,

It depends on the type of man giving the signals. It could be anything from a lack of warmth to never seeking your opinion to belittling. I saw one man solicit an opinion on a new advertisement. He asked several members of his team: "Bob? Julie? Penny?"

Penny said, "Use full color."

The man totally ignored her, and said, "Bob, coming back to you…" This man was sending a clear signal. Anyone who knows what's good for them will begin to avoid her. If he sends even stronger signals, subtly belittling Penny, saying, "When we want to get to that, we will," he's hoping she'll get the hint and leave. The problem comes when she doesn't. If she sees the signal, she should go to him and say, "You know, I'm interested in this other opportunity in the sales department. Can you help?" If he says, "Sure!" that's her next signal. When you get the first signals that your opinion isn't valued, there's time to repair the damage or switch to a different position. Once you feel belittled, it's time to leave the company. We had to coach one woman on my team because she was brilliant, fast, and highly effective, but she scared people. She read the signals early and was open to coaching and totally changed. Her new rankings shot through the roof, from below average to the top 1 percent.

SO WHAT'S A WOMAN TO DO?

Despite the many examples of women mixing the rules of Personal and Work Worlds, it was encouraging to hear from men many examples of female colleagues perfectly in tune with the expectations of the working world. It was also interesting to see the high degree of gratitude and respect these women engendered. A national sales director named Louis said,

> I have ten talented women working for me, and two of them do not let these things [taking things personally] become an issue. As a result, they are extraordinarily valuable to me. I always know what I'm going to get, and I can trust them completely. When women can both bring their skills to the table *and* eliminate the subconscious unknowns or discomfort many men have working with them—just from the unpredictability of it—they are viewed as among the most valuable employees.

Exactly how does a woman do this?

One of the simplest tools for managing men's perceptions is to ask yourself, "Is this what a man would expect to encounter in Work World?" If the answer is no, men suggest, don't let men hear it or see it, especially in secular workplaces, which have even less grace on this issue.

> *"The women who do not let these things become an issue are extraordinarily valuable to me. I always know what I'm going to get, and I can trust them completely."*

Some of the best advice I received early on in my career was from an older, wiser female friend who left a big company and began her own consulting practice. I was at her office late one Thursday afternoon, as we were getting ready to knock off work and head to a church musical rehearsal that night and all the next day. A fellow consultant called her to ask for input on a proposal. She told him,

"Frank, I'm heading out to a meeting now, and I'm in meetings all day tomorrow. I'll look at this over the weekend and get back to you Monday." As she put down the phone, she looked at me and said, "Just so you know: don't ever tell a man in business that you can't do something because of personal commitments. You're in a meeting. He doesn't need to know if that meeting is with your kids' dentist. If he does, he starts to think this irrational thing that you allow personal life to interfere with work. Don't even give him the opportunity to go there."

Every office has its own culture, of course, but whenever you have a choice, it rarely hurts to err on the side of caution. It's worth being aware of how something as simple as seeing a woman apply lipstick at her desk can yank a man back into Personal World.

> Ask yourself, "Is this what a man would expect to encounter in Work World?"

Similarly, while we may not be able to actually eliminate the existence of personal feelings, and our brain structure makes compartmentalizing emotions difficult, we can probably learn to downplay our feelings enough that men don't see them as part of the equation. For example, try to mentally separate yourself from your position, or force yourself to respond calmly when you feel yourself getting upset. Remind yourself, "It's not about me; it's about the other person and *their* perception." Most of us need a place to vent at times. We can do that off site, back in Personal World.

Thankfully, men don't expect us to be exactly like them. For if we are going to apply the perceived rules of the working world to our own work life, we need to do so in a way that works for us, can be sustained over the long term, and allows us to respect ourselves in the process. Geoff, the Fortune 500 CMO, advised,

It is so important for women to understand how men communicate, think, form clubs, and have their own language and expectations. For example, men are hunters. But don't try to break into their clubs and go hunting. Don't try to look like them, *but try to be perceived as compatible to them* [emphasis mine]. If five guys go to Bernie's Bar and you show up, it will look like you're trying too hard. If you happen to see them there, that's okay. But don't jump in with "How about those Packers?" Say, "I notice the *Wall Street Journal* said such-and-such." It's a good icebreaker. Give them a chance to see how good you are.

PERCEIVED AS EQUAL

It is important to emphasize why men expect both men and women to function according to the same rules at work. It is because they view the genders equally. Or to put it another way, men's frustration with women who don't function according to the natural laws of Work World stems in large part from an egalitarian view. Cole, the executive search founder, explained,

There was a time, even fifteen or twenty years ago, when men expected women to approach them differently than other men. There was this expectation, an old school viewpoint, that if a man was going to say something, he would say it one way and a woman would say it another way. Today, I do not expect a woman to treat me any differently than a man. I do not expect to be paternalistic toward a woman, and I do not expect her to defer to me. That's a good thing.

I do view that as a very good thing, and I hope you see it the same way. This doesn't mean that we will always view men's working-world expectations as correct. Regardless, if we can recognize and use these expectations as a means of influence, as a way to develop trust between equals, and as stepping stones to leadership, we can begin to change the culture. Once men see that their understanding of how to do business isn't, in fact, the only way of getting to a successful outcome, they too may become more adaptable.

CHAPTER 2

"She's Crying—What Do I Do?"

How Men View Emotions at Work

After a meeting with a high-level female consultant about the topics addressed in this book, she sent me a small gift wrapped in funky paper. Inside was a notepad by cartoonist Leslie Murray with a snappy female character saying, "Laugh and the world laughs with you. Cry and men have no idea what to do."

I had to chuckle because in my research on men in the workplace, that observation has come across as all too true. And like many women, I have seen that reality in my own professional life, including in an unexpectedly difficult meeting a few years ago.

After *For Women Only* came out, I developed close working relationships with many organizations that help families on the subject of marriage, by sharing research, speaking at their retreats or corporate meetings, and appearing on television or radio broadcasts. Early on, when a few female readers spread the rumor that I was laying all the blame for bad relationships on women (instead of recognizing that I was simply explaining how men think and had written the other side of the story in the men's book), one organization was particularly helpful in using its influence to distribute my research and correct that misunderstanding.

So when I was in their area some time back and several members of a small counseling working group wanted to meet with me, I willingly agreed. But I was blindsided. In disbelief, I listened as several people I respected laid out a list of about twenty inaccurate accusations against my message, concluding that I laid all the blame for bad relationships on women.

It was a long, emotionally exhausting meeting, and I ended up angrily trying to defend myself, shedding tears, then getting angrier that I was presenting myself so poorly.

Thankfully, in the months following, we were able to trace the cause of the problem, correct those misperceptions, and restore the relationship. But for the next year, every time a man in one of my interviews brought up their private perceptions about a woman becoming "emotional," my mind would bounce uncomfortably back to that meeting. I knew how it must have been perceived.

I would guess almost every woman has been in the mortifying situation of becoming emotional in a professional setting, and wishing she could turn back time and do it differently. Or vanish into the floorboards. When I interviewed one vice president of human resources at a large technology company, I asked what women might unintentionally do that hurts their effectiveness with men. The VP laughed, and in one smooth move rolled his chair to the corner of his L-shaped desk, picked up a large box of Kleenex, rolled his chair back, and plonked the box down in front of me. "Do you see this box of Kleenex?" he asked, raising his eyebrows. "If I only worked with men, there would be no box of Kleenex on my desk."

It is no surprise to women that men view emotion as inappropriate in a work setting. After all, we generally do too. But most women don't realize just what men view as "getting emotional" in the first place (it's more than just crying), how negatively most men view it, or how positively they view the worker who handles emotion and other interpersonal issues in ways they see as valid and constructive.

This issue of managing emotion was one of the foremost topics that came up in my interviews. Men clearly thought an inability to manage emotion well was a way talented women shot themselves in the foot. Yet these same men also often commended women for their superior empathetic, listening, and interpersonal skills. In short, many men clearly saw the benefits of someone who was relational but not emotional.

> Most women don't realize just what
> men view as "getting emotional" in
> the first place.

Why is that? And what does "getting emotional" mean to men in the first place? How do men think emotions should be handled, and how can we manage perceptions of ourselves in this area? Let's take a look.

WHY EMOTIONS ARE DIFFICULT FOR MEN

You've probably wondered this countless times in your own relationships with men at work and in your personal life: why, when faced with significant emotion, do men often get that look of a deer in the headlights: part panic and part pain? The reason has to do with the hardwiring of the male brain. I'll explain this briefly, below. If you want to learn more, see the Appendix, "Emotions and the Male Brain," on page 235.

As you know from chapter 1, women are more hardwired for mental multitasking than men, whose mental default is to compartmentalize. Nowhere is this more evident than in how men and women handle emotions. The multitasking female brain seems better wired to process strong emotions and (up to a point) think clearly at the same time. By contrast, the male brain is better designed for more focused, one-thing-at-a-time processing. Thus, the presence of strong emotions makes it more difficult for a man to simultaneously process those emotions and think clearly. And because men can't think as clearly when they are experiencing strong emotion, they often assume women can't either.

In some ways, in other words, emotion furs up the gears in the male brain.

Exacerbating the situation is the fact that the male brain wiring is specifically designed more for action than for picking up subtle, interpersonal cues. One commercial real estate developer compared his attempts to read and handle interpersonal issues as like trying to hit a moving target. That resonated with me. I enjoy those target-shooting games at fairgrounds, but only when the little metal ducks or bunny rabbits are stationary. When they begin to move, I end up shooting wildly and get frustrated, unable to keep up and unable to hit a thing.

This is the feeling men describe when they try to track with emotion. Up to a point, the men say they are fine. After that point, they often feel overwhelmed and like they aren't as well equipped to handle it. And because their brain structure makes them less likely to pick up subtle signals of emotion (such as body language) to begin with, they sometimes end up misreading interpersonal cues or missing them altogether. The inadequate feeling they experience as a result is intensely frustrating—the men told me it is one of the worst feelings they can have. As the real estate developer admitted, "It's uncomfortable not knowing if someone's going to fly off the handle. There is a lot more stress with uncertainty."

So as a result (especially at work), men handle the situation by using their enviable ability to compartmentalize: they essentially shut off emotions to process them later or try to avoid them entirely. In a conversation in an airline club room with two executives, one of them explained, "We're just not that great at the interpersonal stuff sometimes, so it's easier to just ignore it."

His colleague said, "Let me be more blunt. We avoid it *because* we're bad at it! And we know that we are bad at it! You know how we were talking about the 'rules' of the business world that men came up with? And one of those rules was to not be influenced by emotions? Well, we're really smart. One of the rules we created was to not take into account stuff that we're poor at doing!"

WHAT MEN SEE AS GETTING EMOTIONAL

In the course of my research, I was surprised to discover that becoming inappropriately "emotional" actually includes a great deal more than fighting back tears. I have been in each of the situations described below more than once myself. But until I started these interviews, I had no idea that men would have perceived these actions as emotional.

Let's start with what men see as the most obvious sign of emotions on the loose.

Becoming tearful

One high-level Christian businessman said something echoed by many men I interviewed:

> Most women I've worked with at one point or another have cried—say 80 percent, from an officer in the company, to my VP of marketing, down to a secretary. That really throws you off in a workplace. Our natural reaction is to give the woman a hug, but that is not appropriate. So handling that is a challenge. What is the appropriate response? "Go get yourself together"? There's not a whole lot of compassion in that. Privately, I feel exactly like Tom

Hanks's character in the movie *A League of Their Own* when he says, "There's no crying in baseball!" That's sort of the way any guy feels at the office: There's no crying in business!

Becoming upset or defensive

Parallel to crying, men cited getting visibly riled—or defensive, which implies you're upset and trying to cover for it. Kevin, the human resources director for a major consulting firm, told me he had a senior benefits manager working with him who was "fabulous," except for one tendency he found very off-putting:

> Just recently we were in a group meeting discussing benefits packages for our firm in the U.S. and abroad. The benefits manager gave her presentation, then someone asked whether the data included such-and-such or whether we should do additional analysis about a particular factor, basically a "what-if" scenario—"what if we did this?" But in her mind she heard it as, "Why did you not think of this already?" She responded very defensively, saying, "I already tried to do the analysis you are talking about," and, "We do not have the data necessary to do that," and, "The resource I used only had this particular data source. I would have to find other data sources and I do not know where to find them in the time frame you need." She went into a long discussion of why she cannot do what we wanted her to do.

When I asked him what, specifically, made her response seem defensive instead of just an explanation, he said, "She immediately jumped to a defensive tone of voice, and her face got beet red. The whole room was like, 'Okay, settle down. Don't get in a tizzy. This is not an accusation against you.'"

"And yet you describe her as fabulous," I prodded.

"Yes," he said. "She is. She's very, very bright. It's just that she also has this defensiveness. One day I asked her about it, and she said, 'It is just because I desire to please everyone. When I'm questioned like that, I feel they are not pleased, and like I must have done something wrong.'"

How could she have handled it better, or how would a man have handled it differently? "A man will never get mad and emotional like some women," Kevin said. "She almost seemed on the verge of saying, 'Fine,' and storming out. A man would never do that. I would expect a man to say, 'I hear your perspective and respectfully disagree. We can agree to disagree on this, but let me first give you my perspective.' Then I'd expect him to leave it. But I've seen women give off this vibe of just getting so frustrated and emotional, like, 'I cannot deal with this anymore.'"

Other men I spoke with universally described defensiveness as unpleasant. It wasn't that they didn't put up a businesslike defense if they felt their statements or actions were not being properly understood. Rather, men said they rarely heard other men get *defensive*, or as Kevin put it, "frustrated and emotional." Men said they, too, can feel defensive, frustrated, and emotional, but they tend to hide and compartmentalize such turmoil so it is not dealt with until later, and is certainly not seen.

Overreacting, or "making a mountain out of a molehill"

Another commonly mentioned behavior was the perception that women are more likely to blow something out of proportion. The comments of Cole, the executive search leader, come across as somewhat harsh on the page, but his tone was actually just perplexed:

I had a meeting yesterday with a client who is a female executive at a Fortune 500 company, and I had to give her some bad news about a project. I told her our top candidate for a CFO search just took himself out of consideration. My client went, "Aaahh!" Just like that. I said, "It isn't as though I told you that your father just suffered a heart attack, or your son was arrested. It's just business." She said, "I know, but he was our top candidate," and goes on a bit about her disappointment. I hear her, but I am thinking, *This is just business! There's no point in spending a whole hour on the emotional side of things.*

Clearly, the conversation with Cole's client did not take an hour of emotional discourse, but that's what her perceived overreaction felt like to him. I find this notable because even as a more empathetic man, Cole felt that making something into a bigger deal was equivalent to becoming emotional.

As other men shared stories and examples like this, I noted that while they all thought the woman's reaction was irrational, most were reluctant to confront it like Cole. A partner at a major professional services firm explained, "In that situation, the guy says to himself, 'This is so unimportant, but I can't say it is unimportant because it is clearly important to her—for whatever reason.'"

Jumping to conclusions

A number of men felt women were more likely than men to express a knee-jerk reaction to things. That assumption carries with it the belief that the woman's decision making and thinking must be emotion driven and therefore not driven by logic—and here is where the difference in our brain wiring leads to natural tension.

In some situations the extra-multitasking processing power in a woman's brain (all those white-matter superhighways) allows her to do a sort of fast zip-processing of multiple options: assessing X, Y, and Z, and getting an instant sense that Z won't work—and voicing an opinion before her colleagues. But because she doesn't explain her rapid-fire line of reasoning, the men in the room assume that she is jumping to conclusions. So they start saying things like, "Well, hold on a moment, let's not be hasty..."

Further, because male brains aren't as hardwired to pick up on subtle interpersonal cues, they may not have noticed critical factors (such as a client's facial expression) that informed the woman's rapid response.

When asked what women do to undermine their standing with men, one survey taker specifically brought up, "Jumping to a conclusion about a person's motivation or intention based on a brief instant or, for example, a nonverbal motion or communication."

Now, I'm not saying that a woman's instantaneous read is always right, nor that men or women are immune from knee-jerk reactions. But it is critical for women to realize that even when they are accurate in rapid-fire logic, their way of decision making easily can be misperceived by men as emotion driven and therefore suspect.

> *Rapid-fire logic can easily be misperceived as emotion driven and therefore suspect.*

Refusing to be swayed

Another common theme I heard among men, with varying degrees of irritation, was that some women seemed to form stubbornly strong opinions and refused to be swayed. Such women are seen as going beyond the sort of push-back that happens in business disagreements. They are seen as "unable to let it go" and unable to defer to the decision of the boss or the opinion of the group. Such a perception led the men to think of the person in question as irrational and emotional.

One survey taker, when asked what would undermine a man's perception of a woman, said, "If she gets emotional about a project. Some women who are skilled will not listen to others' opinions. They are right about everything and will not discuss or listen to other sides."

Now, most people that I know in business would view someone who was "not listening to others' opinions" as being unprofessional. It is telling that this man—like many others—labeled it as "getting emotional."

Here are a few other survey quotes that show how a woman's tenaciousness can be perceived:

- "She just gets so mad because she's not getting her way."
- "Why can't she wrap her mind around this particular topic? Why can't she see it in another way? Why is she so dead set on being right?"
- "After we told her no, all these people started coming to me and saying, 'We're going to lose the farm over this.' They were all riled up. And we knew it was because of her. She became very emotional and refused to be rational and made an emotional play to others. And she seriously hurt herself with our CEO and others."

Personality conflicts

Because many men are uncomfortable with picking up on or managing interpersonal cues and emotions, they also tend to be uncomfortable with personality conflicts in the workplace. In fact, men tend to dismiss most interpersonal problems as emotion driven and having no place at work. They feel like they should have to spend zero time managing personal conflicts or dealing with fallout, and they resent it when that is not the case.

One businesswoman, Grace, told me of a conflict she had with a new woman who was hired for an influential position in a parallel department. Grace had been in the business for years as the right hand to an extremely busy president. She highly valued the cooperative, family-like environment of the organization. The new woman had a very different style, which Grace felt was brusque, personally demeaning, and deflating to the morale of her own employees and the culture of the entire organization. She became concerned that her employees would leave—or that she would have to. When Grace raised these concerns with the president, however, he was impatient that she even brought it up. Several times he told her, "This is between the two of you. You just have to work it out."

Most of us have been in situations where a certain senior person is extremely difficult to work with and is causing good people to leave, yet the leadership of the organization seems to want to do nothing. At least some of those cases are likely due to the inherent assumptions of male leaders that this is an emotion-based personality conflict, that it has no place at work, and that the individuals involved simply need to work it out and get back to business.

Anything they don't understand

Finally, there is something that men view as emotional that I believe is one of the most insidious and damaging assumptions to women at work, because it is so deeply embedded in the male psyche and so difficult to confront. It is the common, subconscious assumption by men that there is some part of a woman that is random or inscrutable.

From boyhood, many men have come to believe that to one degree or another, women are mysterious, not entirely consistent, and will never be able to be completely understood. Thus, as adults, when confronted with a woman's words or actions that confuse them or seem illogical, they too easily chalk it up to "that random part of her" and look no further.

I've seen this devastate personal relationships, when, for example, a husband sees his wife's unhappiness, doesn't understand the reason for it, and thus assumes there isn't one and that it can't be addressed (instead of assuming there *is* a reason, that maybe it has something to do with him, and that it *can* be addressed). I have come to see that such an assumption can be damaging to women's careers, as well.

I was shocked and sobered at the number of times I asked a man for an example of something he viewed as getting emotional, and was told a story that had nothing to do with emotion that I could see. Instead, it essentially demonstrated that he simply didn't understand the reason for her words or actions. It wasn't that he actively thought she was emotional, but that he didn't understand why she had said or done something. So he chalked it up to random emotion. As one senior executive said,

> With my sales director, you never know what Mary you're going to get. You see this much more in women than you do in men. Men are just more consistent that way. If they are jerks, they're jerks. You know what sort of situations trigger it. If you do X, you get that reaction. Here, you never knew why the female marketing director or sales director would get offended. It was always potluck.

WHEN YOUR EMOTIONS SHOW UP, HERE'S WHAT HE THINKS

So when men see emotion, how do they view it? It's no surprise that they view it as unprofessional. But we may not realize that they often hold other, equally damaging perceptions as well. Here are some of their common assumptions when they see someone "getting emotional."

"This person is not thinking"

As one man put it, "The moment I see someone tearing up, I think, 'There goes the logical part of this conversation. We can now abandon logic.' Men think if someone is crying, they've ceased to be logical."

While a particularly intense flood of emotion makes it difficult for anyone to think clearly, science shows that women's emotional threshold is, in essence, much higher than men's. Women can experience strong feelings and still be able to think clearly, but because men usually can't, they think women can't either. To men, emotion *is* irrational in many ways. Aidan, a change management partner at a global consulting firm, gave an example:

> Kelly, on my team, is extremely talented but so sensitive. She and I went to a sixteen-person meeting last week. The client, a major airline going through massive change, invited four competing consulting companies to sit in one room and lay out ideas for how to handle it. We all knew we were competing for the whole job or part of the job, and our role was to run the meeting, make a first pass, and suggest a starting point.
>
> Kelly was so angry that everyone else in the room was dinging our ideas and that we were being criticized, that she said nothing the whole meeting. She and I were the only ones there from our firm, and it was odd that she wouldn't chip in. So I couldn't rely on her take on anything that happened in the meeting, because she was so emotional about it.

Notice Aidan's assumption path: The fact that Kelly was angry led to her becoming inappropriately silent. The fact that she was silent meant she was being emotional. The belief that she was emotional meant (he assumed) that she wasn't thinking clearly, and thus that he couldn't rely on her judgment about anything that happened in the meeting.

I heard so many similar stories from other men that I included that exact scenario on my survey. I asked what men would think if a female colleague became "emotional and upset" by criticism of a team project. I also asked men how they would react as they reviewed such a meeting—would they assume a woman wasn't thinking clearly and doubt her judgment?

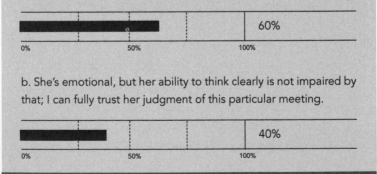

Now suppose that you are leaving the meeting in which your female colleague was emotional and upset. As you prepare to review the meeting, what thought is most likely to be your first reaction? (Choose one answer.)

a. She's emotional, so unfortunately she's probably not thinking very clearly right now; it casts a doubt over whether I can trust her judgment of this particular meeting.

60%

0%   50%   100%

b. She's emotional, but her ability to think clearly is not impaired by that; I can fully trust her judgment of this particular meeting.

40%

0%   50%   100%

Six men out of ten surveyed said they would assume the emotional colleague wasn't thinking clearly and that they couldn't trust her judgment of the meeting. As the men's second assumption about emotion makes clear (below), I suspect the real-life percentage of men who might think that is even higher.

"This 'not thinking' will be catching"

Because men find themselves starting to feel out of balance when they encounter strong emotion, they assume everyone else in the room will be too. Their real fear is that emotion will cloud everyone's thinking and decision making. One nonprofit marketing manager said,

> On the squash court, emotion is one thing. We can holler and get passionate, and it's infectious. That is okay. But when emotion infects a work meeting, it makes me feel really uncomfortable; I'm not 100 percent focused and I've got this jangling going on inside, and other people do too. I begin to fear I'll have to have that same meeting on another day when people aren't getting emotional because what's getting done isn't getting done correctly.

Another senior business leader said,

> When I see emotion in the room, my first feeling is true empathy for that person because they are going through some trauma. My second feeling is concern. It is the feeling you get when you're driving and realize that the car next to you is driving straight on and is not looking at the red light in front of them. It's a car wreck about to happen. To watch somebody conduct themselves in a way that could ultimately be destructive to their own best interests is just really a sad thing.

Here is how I asked the initial question on the survey.

Suppose you are in an important meeting that you know you and your team will need to evaluate afterward. One of your female colleagues contributes well to the discussion but also gets quite emotional and upset about some criticism of your team's project. Which of the following feelings are you most likely to have?
(Choose one answer.)

a. I fear that her emotion could draw others into it, and make it a more emotional, less productive meeting.

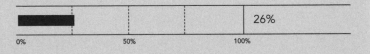

b. I agree with (a), above, and as a result feel I would need to filter the emotional stuff out so I can think clearly.

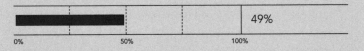

c. I don't fear the meeting becoming more emotional; if it did, it wouldn't impact me at all.

In other words, three out of four of the men I surveyed were fearful that emotion would infect the meeting and make it unproductive. Most of those men say they have to actively filter out the emotion in order to think clearly themselves. Given these numbers, it is likely that the response to the question we looked at earlier—whether women who became emotional in a meeting would or would not be able to think clearly—was artificially suppressed by concern over how the answer would be perceived.

"This person is missing things"

A parallel to the "she's not thinking" assumption is the belief that if she's emotional, she's missing what's happening here and now. Aidan, the change management partner, gave a powerful example:

FROM A PARTNER AT A GLOBAL CONSULTING FIRM

When you're a consultant at a client site, working with twenty of their people in a conference room, some of them won't like the consultant running things. That's their issue, not yours; get on with it. But I've seen that sometimes some women want so much to be liked that I really get the feeling that they are thinking to themselves, "These people wish I wasn't running the meeting," and get distracted by it. These women are actually reading the situation very well, but are not able to just ignore that distraction and get on with the job. Their concern gets in the way because they end up missing some of what is going on, not hearing what is being said.

A few months ago, a senior member of my team and I had a key meeting with [a major soft-drink company]. There were tensions in the room. Some people didn't think we, as outsiders, should be involved. Laurie was supposed to lead parts of the meeting, but she got so focused on those in the room who didn't like us. I could tell she was getting defensive toward the people in the room for some reason. And it turned out later, they didn't even have an issue with us, but with whether the project needed to be done in the first place.

Laurie could have just addressed it and said, "It seems you aren't in agreement here, let's talk about it." But because she was defensive about their questioning, she kept pushing our point of view and agenda really hard and didn't listen well to them at all. And ironically, it was *because* she was emotionally intelligent and knew that their body language was bad that she picked up on their reservations at all! I honestly didn't see it. But she assumed those reservations were because they didn't want us there. And instead it was that they had reservations about the project. And those would have been really important to hear!

We did go ahead with the project and unfortunately found out what the problems were as we went, but not through her. And that means we have reservations about her running a meeting again.

"About crying..."

It's important to emphasize that although the aforementioned negative perceptions were shared by most men about all the different types of emotion, some men were more generous than others when the situation actually involved tears. One senior analyst I've known for years told me, "It's true that women are the only ones who ever get teary-eyed at work. But I don't think we look down on women for being women, especially if the tears aren't about intrusive personal stuff, a regular drama, or meant to manipulate."

But unfortunately, some men did clearly look down on anyone who cried at work, even if they mentally accommodated it. As Tyler, an entertainment company EVP, told me, "I've worked in this business for twenty-five years, and I've had many women in my office, crying. That hasn't happened with a single man. And I just deal with it. But privately, I don't have patience for it. It's counterproductive. All it does is create gossip and fodder for everyone to talk about. It's pointless."

Many men told me tears at work were "pointless," clearly not recognizing that the woman isn't trying to bring them in on purpose! I must confess that internally, I was often dying to say, *"It's pointless? Oh my goodness—I guess we'll stop doing it, then."*

> **Many men told me tears at work were "pointless." I was often dying to say, "It's pointless? Oh my goodness—I guess we'll stop doing it, then."**

And that, of course, leads us to the big question.

WHAT DO WE DO ABOUT IT?

When I worked at the New York Fed, I always marveled at how calm my immediate boss was in the midst of even the most nerve-wracking situation. He was an assistant vice president, managing more than one dozen stressed-out analysts on deadlines often measured in minutes. Early on, I would run into his office holding a draft memo for him to review and correct, knowing that his boss, the executive vice president, needed it to brief the president in twenty minutes. Even though two or three other analysts were usually hustling in and out on similar missions, my boss always projected an ultracalm front. He would very deliberately scan my paper, hand back his red-penned corrections, and calmly reach for the next anxious analyst's paper as I ran out.

After a while, I stopped running. I realized the more strung out we got, the more calm he got, and that his demeanor was an excellent strategy to reduce tension and keep things moving efficiently. I also realized that the more stressed I appeared, the longer he took to review my work. Now I realize that was because he assumed I was missing things.

Eventually I and other staff members started copying his calm demeanor. Today, my own staff members sometimes wonder aloud how I can be so calm when I'm on a tight deadline or thrown a curveball. (Although as the example earlier in this chapter shows, I'm still working on that.)

One investment banker perfectly summarized my boss's behavior—and the advice I heard from many men on how they think emotions should be handled at work:

Men have emotions too, but they harness those emotions. I don't want to be manipulative, but you can generate the right emotion around the topic, in order to create value toward your goal instead of allowing an unproductive emotion to naturally flow from the circumstances.

He gave this example:

If a client calls me and says, "We are going to give you this big project," my initial emotion is, "Yippee!" But I don't say that to my client. None of us would. We'll say, "Excellent. We can be out there tomorrow." We hang up the phone, and *then* we high-five it with our colleagues. We restrain our emotions. But women sometimes don't restrain their emotions. When a key employee comes in and says, "I cannot handle it here anymore; I quit," an ineffective response is to show upset emotions. If I say, "Quit! What do you mean, quit? Think of all the things I have done for you!" that does not help solve the problem. In fact, it is almost always an ineffective solution, for either gender, to show negative emotions. It will just solidify a decision we don't want. So the right response is to harness these emotions and say, "I understand the job has been killing you recently, and you're feeling less than appreciated. The last few years, I tried to show you appreciation, but for the last three or four months, I have absolutely failed to do that. Whether you go or stay, I want to tell you right now how sorry I am." That approach restrains negative emotions and tries to create value instead.

This investment banker reminds us that men experience the same feelings as women but just find it easier to compartmentalize those emotions. Also, he believed women could be equally or more effective at restraining and redirecting emotions to create value. Based on my experience with my boss at the Fed, I think it is a matter of being aware of and purposeful about it.

> "Men have emotions too, but they harness those emotions. You can generate the right emotion instead of allowing an unproductive emotion to naturally flow from the circumstances."

Addressing the negative way men view emotion in the workplace can be done in two ways: working to manage the emotions themselves, or managing men's perceptions.

Managing emotion

One business owner, referred to as unusually sensitive and empathetic by a venture capitalist who knows him, offered this helpful perspective:

Men or women who cannot disassociate themselves from the emotional trauma of business end up leaving it or failing. But disassociating yourself does not mean you do not feel or do not care. It means you do not let your actions stem from an emotional response, and you do not let any outward show of your emotions hinder the agenda you are trying to accomplish. What is even more important is changing what emotions you show.

Most people are willing to edit their words. We learn that we should think before we talk so we do not always say everything we are thinking. In the business context that edit function is really important. But some people don't have the same ability to edit their emotions, so in some instances they show emotions that are not particularly advantageous to the agenda they are trying to accomplish.

I would argue that his last point—not showing negative emotions when it would put us at a disadvantage—is the most critical. But how do we do that? I asked that of one business owner after I shared my opening story of becoming emotional when faced with unexpected accusations from presumed allies. He advised,

> It is analogous to what a politician does. Politicians know they will get antagonistic questions about beliefs and policies very important to them—comments that are always a surprise and very personal. So they prepare ahead of time for how they might answer various scenarios. I think most guys do that: They prepare mental scripts. I'm betting that since that situation, you have scripted over and over in your head how you wished you would have handled it differently.

"Of course," I responded, "but part of the problem was that I never would have expected to be criticized in that meeting. If I'm expecting a tough meeting, scripts are doable. What happens when it's unexpected?" His answer:

When our daughters were little, they played softball, and the coach told them, "When the ball is hit to the outfield, always take your first step back." Their inclination is to take their first step forward and run toward it, but by that time they cannot really adjust and the ball is over their heads. This is like that. No matter what comes at me, I always take my first step back emotionally. I've learned that I have to give myself space to think and get my emotions under control. If you had to do it over again, you might have scripted your remarks by listening to the criticism, then asking for a few minutes to process what was said and think it through. Or you could say, "Let's establish some common ground. Obviously there are strong opinions in the room about what I've written. I want to share what my intentions were, and hear what you think they were."

I've found his advice about taking a step back helpful. As the business owner added, "Your first goal is to pull the fuse off the stick of dynamite in the room so it does not explode. Your second goal is to give yourself a chance to respond in a way that is rational and can add some benefit to the situation rather than in an emotional way that does not. It will help to plan to do that whenever you are blindsided. That becomes your script."

> "Give yourself a chance to respond in a way that is rational and can add some benefit to the situation rather than in an emotional way that does not."

Managing perceptions

As I've drilled down into the advice from men, there are two main ways that women can manage men's perceptions so that they don't see us as emotional, even when we wrestle with those emotions inside. The first entails what I call forced calmness. The second requires being very aware of possible misperceptions and taking rapid, preventative action.

Forced calmness. From all accounts, it seems as if the best thing women can do when we feel ourselves getting upset is project a facade of calm. This has dual benefit: it pulls the fuse out of the stick of dynamite, and it helps us start to feel the inner peace we project. As Geoff, the Fortune 500 CMO quoted earlier, said, "Women at senior levels have to understand that sometimes men overreact big too. And women can't overreact to that overreaction. Remember, he'll be done in ten minutes and won't think about it the rest of the day."

I should note that projecting an attitude of calmness does not mean actually becoming callous or filtering out emotions so ruthlessly that we eliminate our natural strength in interpersonal dynamics. One man articulated this: "There is a risk of trying to compartmentalize too much when that doesn't come naturally—like the women who come in and entirely de-emotionalize every situation. And so they rip people to shreds and do not understand why there is this carnage in their wake. And everybody is just waiting for them to fall down an elevator shaft."

Taking rapid corrective action. Since women are particularly well equipped to notice subtle unspoken cues (like body language), we are well placed to be able to be aware of the signs that men think we are getting emotional—and demonstrate that we're not. For example, when we suspect that a negative perception may be arising ("She's getting too upset—I'll bet she's missing things"), we can move to counter it ("Listen, I know I'm passionate about this, but Bob, you just made points A, B, and C, and here's why I'm concerned about how B might work..."). Specifically addressing incorrect assumptions is vital.

I saw this in my second year at Harvard's Kennedy School. I was one of two graduate students from my program appointed to be a full member of the admissions committee. One of the most valuable lessons I learned is that in the absence of information, an observer has to make an assumption. If the situation is a negative one (your GPA slipped your senior year), that assumption is probably not to your benefit ("This guy was slacking off"). But if you move to provide an explanation ("My mother passed away my senior year, and I had to help with my younger siblings"), the negative assumption is countered or never gets made in the first place—and is often turned into a positive ("Wow, this is a responsible guy").

It works the same way in managing any perceptions, including with men in the workplace. For example, it is worth keeping a particularly close eye on situations where women might be assumed to be jumping to conclusions. One of my close friends is a female consultant in a largely male-dominated field, and she is usually tapped as the team leader. She found that when she states an opinion, there's no problem if the men on her team immediately are on board with her viewpoint. But if she senses they aren't, she has to make a point of sitting down with them and sharing the steps of her reasoning so they follow what otherwise might seem a hasty, instinctive process.

Similarly, it is worth being aware of situations where a man might assume women are being dragged into an interpersonal conflict. To demonstrate otherwise, it helps for a woman to explain the business impact of the situation and recommend what to do about it.

Now, obviously, many men will immediately grasp the importance of issues that impact morale. But if a woman raises concern about (for example) a peer's brusque approach with her employees and is told, "You just have to work it out between the two of you," she clearly is not being understood and has to shift strategies.

I relayed that exact example to one retired banker who suggested instead,

> You will absolutely catch any leader's attention if you start
> with the fact that the situation is affecting performance.
> Is quality down? Is the morale problem affecting service
> delivery? Is productivity affected? If it's just complaining
> and whining, then forget it—you just have to work it out.
> But if it's affecting performance, it's a different deal.

Obviously, many men care just as much about interpersonal dynamics and morale, will have seen the same signals, and therefore won't need this approach. But if you're getting the feeling that your male boss may not be seeing the same things you are, it makes sense to use the approach least likely to be labeled an emotional one.

TURNING PERCEIVED WEAKNESS TO STRENGTH

No doubt men will continue to view women as more emotional, and in truth, given our hardwiring, we are. That is not a bad thing. God created each of us the way He did for a reason. The key to success for men and women is to leverage those strengths while recognizing and compensating for areas that could negatively impact how we're perceived. Clearly, a woman's relatively more complex emotional wiring is an example of both. As Cole said,

> What makes a great executive is somebody who can get
> emotional about the needs of their subordinates and peers,
> but does not get emotional about their own needs. And
> where women may at times fail is that they become

emotional around their own needs and less emotional around the needs of others. But it doesn't always happen that way, obviously. Many women already tend to have a high relational ability that serves them well; those women who also manage emotion well can be very, very effective.

CHAPTER 3

"If I Let Down My Guard, the World Will Stop Spinning"

The Hidden Fear That Drives Men at Work

We've seen that men tend to share common expectations about how the business world works. And I've tried to show you that these defining expectations often stem from male-female differences in the brain, as well as certain instinctive or social predispositions. But there is another factor in play.

I first became aware of it in researching my first book about relationships, *For Women Only*. I was interviewing a small group of men at a coffee shop. The men were talking about how compulsive they felt about the need to provide for their families, and how often—even in an economic boom—they would think or worry about their jobs and their ability to bring home a paycheck.

I asked, "What makes that mental pressure to provide for your family worse?" I listened, confused, as they shared examples of seemingly minor, unrelated work issues. One man talked about a colleague who took too long to get to the point in her explanations; another mentioned an error in a key spreadsheet that required hours to redo; another described an interoffice squabble between two key employees. When I admitted that I didn't get what these things had to do with the topic under discussion, one man tried to elaborate:

Any interruption at work feels like it might prevent me from being able to provide for my family. I know that sounds crazy. While my direct reports are arguing with each other in a meeting, I'm thinking, *Don't you get it? While you're fussing about something irrelevant, my work is not getting done! And if my work is not done, I'm going to lose this client and my numbers will drop. And if my numbers drop, I'm going to get fired. And if I get fired, I'm going to go bankrupt, and I won't be able to provide for my family and my wife will leave me and the glaciers will melt and the world will stop spinning on its axis, and life on earth will cease to exist as we know it.*

The other men laughed and nodded in recognition. "Yep," said one. "That about describes it."

Although men pride themselves on being rational and unemotional, the truth is that both genders have plenty of irrationality to go around. Both women and men have issues that trigger deep emotions—they just tend to be different ones. And as irrational as men know it is, most of the men in my survey shared a visceral fear that their working world might shortly come crashing down if they—and those around them—don't focus all their energy on being productive all the time. In fact, 80 percent agreed with the statement "If everyone doesn't pull together and keep things moving forward every single day, things will break down."[1]

> *Both women and men have issues that trigger deep emotions—they just tend to be different ones.*

Don't miss what to me is the distinctive phrase in that statement—"every single day." Which suggests that the answer to how often men struggle with deep-seated worry about providing for their families is…all the time.

A pastor explained it to me this way: "For men, it goes all the way back to Eden. When Adam disobeyed, God told him, 'You'll always feel this pressure. You'll always feel like the land is fighting against you.' And today, the rest of us feel it, too." As one man put it, "If I don't bust my rear today, I may be bankrupt tomorrow. We know it's stupid, so you'll never hear us talk about it, but that is kind of how every guy feels."

> "If I don't bust my rear today, I may be bankrupt tomorrow."

It was clear in my interviews with men that many, perhaps most, of their work expectations and perceptions can be traced back to this rarely expressed but very real fear.

On one long airplane ride, an engineering company manager had agreed to take a look at a list of ten findings about men I had tentatively developed and was continuing to test. The first hypothesis listed on the paper I handed him was the one that eventually led to this chapter. It was labeled "The World Will Stop Spinning." Other hypotheses on the list included statements about "it's not personal; it's business," how men view emotions, and the importance of "letting it go."

My seatmate read down the list, then handed the pages back and tapped the "world stops spinning" statement. He said,

Just so you know, all but two of your subjects are because of this first one. The reason men value letting it go is because they feel like if they don't, they'll be bankrupt tomorrow. The reason we have all these *Robert's Rules of Order* for the business world is that if we don't, disorder and entropy will take over and we'll soon be out on the street. Anytime a man says, "This is just the way business works," you can bet that this fear is behind it.

But I had still more to learn. I had expected to find that this fear would be most prevalent among white-collar workers, particularly the business owners and principals who carry the ultimate responsibility for the business. I had also, unfortunately, stereotyped blue-collar workers as more likely to have a sense of just putting in their hours. But my survey results found that this fear exists at roughly the same rates whether the men were blue collar or white collar, old or young, company presidents or part-time administrative help, and across the entire occupational spectrum. The slight differences, in fact, were often counterintuitive to my stereotypes. For example, blue-collar workers were actually slightly more likely to feel this concern than white-collar men. (As far as I can tell, if a man doesn't have this fear, it seems more related to working in a system that significantly decreases the need for it—for example, working in a large bureaucratic organization that protects underperformers and doesn't particularly reward those who excel.)

ANATOMY OF A MAN'S FEAR

So how do men experience this hidden fear, and where exactly does it come from? My research indicates that it is rooted in four instinctive feelings or assumptions that men share:

1. The natural order of things is to break down

The engineering company manager I referenced earlier used a word that seemed to perfectly describe the physics behind the men's feelings: *entropy*. One law of thermodynamics essentially states that the universe is running down: no new energy is created, decay happens, things tend to break down and need to be fixed—they don't spontaneously fix themselves. As one definition puts it, entropy is "a measure of the disorder of a system. Systems tend to go from a state of order (low entropy) to a state of maximum disorder (high entropy)."[2]

Men feel this strongly in the working world, and they feel very pressured by it. Left to its own devices, they feel, their area of responsibility will quickly decay or break down. As noted, eight in ten men experienced that feeling.

As one company president, Richard, put it, "A guy has a view that if he doesn't kill himself today, he might be bankrupt tomorrow. It's all part of why we're performance oriented. The natural course of events is for things to break or decay, and if I'm not hard at work reaching goals and ensuring we're on task, we're likely to be broke tomorrow."

2. Constant vigilance is required

That fear of breakdowns naturally leads to the deep, instinctive belief that constant vigilance is needed and that they can never truly relax. I was surprised when I heard this comment from an extremely successful and wealthy businessman: "No matter how successful I get, I still feel a bit like I'm pushing a rock uphill—gravity is still there, working against me. I have to be vigilant or I'll slip backwards."

When I shared that comment on the survey, three out of four men said they felt exactly the same way.

Similarly, 76 percent of the men surveyed agreed with the comment "I feel like a juggler who is trying to keep a dozen balls in the air; if I lose my focus it will all come crashing down around me."

Now, just because a man believes that constant vigilance or focus is needed doesn't necessarily mean he will look like it. As we'll see in another chapter, most men hate looking like they aren't in control. And no one wants to work constantly, every minute of the day. Yet even when a man is socializing at work, or joking with a colleague about last night's game, or relaxing at home on the weekend, he never really feels fully off the hook. As one man put it, "There is always that low-grade buzz in the back of my mind: *What happens if I lose that customer? What happens if my industry tanks? Will my company make it? Will I be able to provide for my family?*"

> "No matter how successful I get, I still feel a bit like I'm pushing a rock uphill—gravity is still there, working against me. I have to be vigilant or I'll slip backwards."

An attorney explained it this way: "Most men have this internal pressure. They don't want to be in work mode every second, but when they aren't, they mentally know there is a trade-off. I'm having a little fun right now, but I know I'm going to have to pay for it later."

3. Even success doesn't provide much breathing room

Recognizing that low-grade buzz or need to keep the pressure on helps to explain why the workplace (a male-dominated one in particular) seems so attuned to the question, "What have you done for me lately?"

I've often thought of that dynamic as counterproductive. Yet it must seem entirely logical in the face of men's conviction that one is always fighting the tendency of things to decay. Seventy-five percent of the men on the survey agreed, saying that even workplace success doesn't give them much breathing room to relax. It's a feeling that was perfectly captured by a comment I heard years ago from an old friend of my husband, a very successful independent financial advisor. He described how he would land a big deal or make $25,000 in one transaction, and his wife would say, "Let's go out and celebrate!" To which he would answer, "How can I celebrate? Now I'm unemployed. I have to go find the next deal!"

4. "It all depends on me"

Throughout my professional life I have heard men say jokingly, "It all depends on me, baby." But as the men in my interviews described it, it's really not a joke.

Almost 85 percent of the men on my survey agreed that they regularly or sometimes felt that everything depended on them. As one of my male advisors put it, "We say, 'It all depends on me,' but what we actually mean is, 'The weight of the world is on my shoulders.'" Now, most of us—men and women—have at times felt that if you want something done right, you've got to do it yourself. It's a feeling that usually rears its head when one is unsure of the competency or commitment of others on the team. But the sense of the men I talked to went deeper than that. It was a feeling men seemed to have even when they had a strong team and were completely confident in those around them.

> "We say, 'It all depends on me,' but what we actually mean is, 'The weight of the world is on my shoulders.'"

Just as success doesn't give men breathing room, the presence of skilled co-workers doesn't remove the lonely, illogical feeling a man has that the weight of the world is on his shoulders, and that he can't truly depend on anyone other than himself to hold it up.

One Christian COO put it this way: "It's fear. It's not that 'I'm so important' and feeling like I have to be the center of things. It's the opposite of that. Now, I know that ultimate responsibility really is the Lord's, not mine. And I know I can trust Him. But I also think men are created to feel the burden to provide, and that pressure is all part of it."

HOW WE ADD TO THAT INTERNAL PRESSURE

While nothing completely eliminates men's fear that their world will stop spinning if they let down their guard, several factors (I'll describe them as Red Flags) definitely increase a man's worry that a colleague doesn't "get it"—which then makes the pressure or fear even worse.

Obviously, these perceptions may be completely inaccurate, fueled solely by a man's underlying "the world will stop spinning" worry. But we can't counter them until we know what they are.

Red Flag 1: "My colleague seems to be prioritizing relationships over results"

As the business leader above noted, any astute worker—man or woman—likely wants to see that those around them are achieving results. But while men viewed women as just as likely to care about achieving results themselves, they were not as convinced that women were as likely to prioritize results in others. A number of men expressed a concern that female managers might preserve a relationship with another worker over results. And that raised the red flag that the woman manager might not share the same fear that the world could come crashing down.

In an earlier chapter, I quoted Marty and Ronald, the CEO and COO of a $5.5 billion organization. After years spent modernizing the company and advancing women, Marty still saw a dynamic that troubled him:

MARTY: For men, performance speaks for itself. They want to be respected on the basis of what they do, not by being able to incur favor. In other words, you do not want to be advancing because someone likes you more than someone else, but because they perceive that you have greater worth.

RONALD: We want our actions to speak for themselves.

I asked both men whether that meant they thought "actions speaking for themselves" mattered more to men than to women.

MARTY: I think so. Because with many women, what I truly see valued is relationship over actions. It is a peculiar thing, because they will be more tolerant of inappropriate actions or substandard delivery to preserve a relationship. The man will usually cut loose a nonperformer much more quickly than a woman. A man may find that easier. It doesn't matter that he may have some existing relationship with that person. With women, I think it does matter.

RONALD: With men, I frankly think we care too little about the relationship. We default back to being just completion driven, outcome driven, so everything doesn't fall apart. We're neurotic cavemen. And someone's got to bring home the mastodon.

Now, clearly, there may be some factor in play in the women's judgment that the men aren't recognizing as related to performance. For example, the women managers they reference may have perceived a business value in prioritizing a relationship. As always, the key for women is to be aware of how men may be perceiving certain actions, so we can proactively address any misperception, if necessary.

Red Flag 2: "My colleague is slowing things down"

Just as men are sometimes unfairly predisposed to see women managers valuing relationships over results, they are predisposed to see certain female approaches to the workplace as more likely to slow down the drive toward results. Men who feel like the world is about to stop spinning get impatient quickly with anything they view as likely to interfere with their ability to keep it moving.

The most common examples I heard were of female colleagues who "slow things down" via some of the patterns discussed elsewhere in this book. For example, allowing emotion to get in the way of business; taking things too personally; sharing too many details instead of getting quickly to the point; or allowing themselves to get enmeshed in interoffice squabbles. In most cases, it was telling that my interviewees viewed these things as not just irritating, but irrelevant to an alarming degree. Several reasonable and even-keeled businessmen became quite passionate about this, revealing how much they view it as an encumbrance to getting the work done. As one normally calm senior executive memorably told me, "It makes you crazy when the two women down the hallway are sniping at each other and I'm like, 'What!? We're going to be broke tomorrow! Go get that report out, make that phone call, get me that next client!'"

Red Flag 3: "My colleague doesn't take the work burden as seriously as I do"

After I described the premise of this chapter to Allan, a Christian leader and president of an automotive industry supply company, he provided an interesting perspective:

Look, not everyone feels that the world will stop spinning if they let down their guard—but if they don't feel that way, I can't trust them to be an effective person or part of my team. If they don't have that same neurosis, I don't think they are taking it seriously enough. We're looking for people who are going to take it as seriously as we do. And when you see someone who doesn't, you think, "I gotta get this guy out of here. He's killing us."

Red Flag 4: "My colleague is doing the job but is not part of the team"

Allan also offered an example that captures the viewpoint of many men who feel the need to keep the world spinning every moment—and shows the value placed on signaling that one is not just doing the job, but is part of the team. His candid recollection is lengthy but may be particularly helpful for any woman needing flexibility in her schedule:

Men recognize skill. But anyone who comes into a new situation would also do well to understand the workplace dynamic and seek some feedback on "am I fitting into it" *before* people start getting concerned behind the scenes and think you're not a team player. Because then you'll have to perform even more. It's like jumping a hurdle: There's always going to be a certain performance threshold or skill set that you are expected to meet. But if you don't comprehend the workplace dynamic and you operate outside of it, you've started by digging yourself a hole—so now you're on an even worse footing and have to jump even higher to meet expectations. And no one needs negative help like that.

I hired a new woman executive a year ago, and she's dynamite—but she got off on the wrong foot. We hired her because we needed someone to help us network into sales calls at a higher level. We're a bunch of engineers and we have a certain way of approaching people—we're not smooth. She's not the same sort of engineer and will never be able to do the same technical stuff, but she is used to working with higher-level people. And that is the skill set I hired her for.

She knew we had a relatively flexible workplace, which she needed to be able to pick her kids up after school. And she said she would work from home instead. We were okay with that. But then there were all these school days off, when she couldn't come in. And then one of the kids was having doctor's visits, or there were special trips, so she would be gone for hours in the middle of the day, or not in at all. And she never asked enough questions about how this fit into our workplace dynamic or what people were thinking.

It's hard to see how hard someone is working from her home office. At first, we thought she wasn't listening to us because she was operating outside even our usual flexible parameters. So the buzz in the office was, "She's taking advantage of how flexible we are." And then there was this office chitchat, so then I was annoyed that she was distracting everyone to the point that their chitchat about her not getting her work done meant that they weren't getting their work done either!

Finally, we had to actually sit down and talk to her, and have the conversation of, "Look, we're here in our expectations—and you're way over here."

That friction lasted until recently, when she started

delivering these huge wins. For example, she just got us a meeting with someone we've been wanting to get in front of for two years. So now all the guys in the office recognize her skill and they are ecstatic. Results-oriented people are always watching to see whether anything is falling through the cracks. But now her fantastic deliverables have proven that nothing is falling through the cracks and have redeemed her lack of time commitment in the office. The men can accept even operating outside the workplace dynamic when they see these huge results.

We now realize that what she has to get done for work has never been sacrificed for her personal schedule. Now that the guys see her big results, they now recognize that she's never said, "I can't call so-and-so because of my kids." But it took us awhile to see that, because we felt that she was always gone.

It would have been so much better to not have to sit her down and say, "You need to rein this in," and instead have *her* ask, "How are things going? What do I need to do to gain everyone's confidence?" And that would have given me a chance to say what any manager would love to be able to say in that situation: "I want you to learn our expectations quickly, because we have a vested interest in making you successful."

SHARING THE BURDEN, EASING THE FEAR

As you can tell by now, men believe that every person in the workplace is constantly being scrutinized to see if he or she is sharing the weight of the world and helping to relieve the common pressure. One survey taker's top advice for talented women was, "Remember that you are being watched and observed by others." And the men I interviewed largely sensed that other men instinctively understood that fact. But rightly or wrongly, men often weren't as sure whether a female colleague realized that reality or valued the need to relieve that pressure. As a result, they felt all the more respectful of women who visibly signaled that they did.

What do these signals look like? I heard so many men talk about these signals that I could have written a chapter on each of them—that is how emotionally important they seemed to be. When someone exhibits both of these characteristics, it makes men think that that person "gets it." Such a person—man or woman—engenders strong feelings of respect and gratitude.

Let's briefly look at them in more detail.

Positive Signal 1: You show you are focused on results—for yourself and others

Ultimately, the best antidote for the fear that things will break down is seeing tangible results that things are moving forward. I can't count the number of men who said, "It's all about results," or, "The only thing that really matters to us is, 'Do you deliver?'" Interestingly, this was usually said in the context of explaining that, in today's workplace, skilled and talented women can advance as fast and as far as similarly skilled men if they focus on delivering results. As one man on the survey put it, "Gender is irrelevant—be competent."

One very successful founder of several nationwide businesses provided an interesting, if blunt, perspective from his four decades in the marketplace:

Early on, I think some women in the 1970s and 1980s—
and even the government—felt that women deserved

different treatment from men. It was business suffrage: I was downtrodden, so now I'm entitled. Business owners used to have to promote a woman primarily *because* she was a woman. I used to have to fill out these government forms stating all the minorities and women I had hired and present a plan for improving my ratio.

That process didn't last long, because the best grand equalizer happens to be capitalism. Today, if you can deliver, it doesn't matter who you are or what race or gender you are.

Capability trumps everything else. And similarly, I can like you a lot as a person, but it doesn't mean I'll hire you or keep you if you haven't earned it. Every business leader today—man or woman—will hire and promote those who perform, period. Because if they don't, they know they won't be around long.

Positive Signal 2: You show you are fully committed—"all in" with the team

Every one of us knows that results matter. But we would be making a big mistake to think that results are *all* that matter. Despite the number of men who said, "It's all about results," those same men shared examples of another aspect of business that I think is vitally important to them: the intangible sense that the other worker is fully committed to the team and equally sharing the unspoken weight on their shoulders.

Understanding how to demonstrate that sense of being "all in" is one of the most overlooked ways a woman can create a deep sense of loyalty among her male colleagues. Several attitudes and behaviors told the men that another employee was taking the job just as seriously as they were:

You make an effort to learn and adapt to the culture and rules of your particular workplace. Essentially, the person is telling the group that he or she understands and respects the unwritten rules of the organization's culture.

> Every one of us knows that results matter. But we would be making a big mistake to think that results are all *that* matter.

In my interview with Allan, the automotive industry supplier, he uttered the classic "performance is what matters" viewpoint. But as you saw earlier, he also gave me an example of a valuable and highly results-oriented new female executive who still created a negative impression. When I pressed him, here's how he explained it:

> Well…it's not *just* the results that matter. You are also expected to work within the office dynamic. You can't have the attitude of "I'm getting my job done, so the other stuff doesn't matter." Especially if you are new and have a learning curve coming in—and so you probably aren't able to deliver immediately—you have to watch out. In every company I've been with, there is a dynamic and a culture that you need to work within. Men are usually fairly cognizant of it. But it's been my impression that women don't care as much about the dynamic as long as they are getting their job done. That is going to be to their detriment, at least in the eyes of the men. If you really want to be accepted by the team and if you really want to move up, don't just deliver the results: Figure out what the rules are and work with them.

In demanding jobs or during demanding times, you make it clear you share the same pain as everyone else. I will cover this point and the next one more extensively in chapter 5, but they're worth mentioning here as signals of someone who is willing to "share the weight of the world."

From their days sweating it out together during two-a-day practices in full gear at summer football camp (or whatever the sport), men create a sense of teamwork and commitment by sharing the same discomfort. No high-school star would say, "Coach, this is crazy. I'm going to skip these pointless extra practices. What matters is whether I can catch the long bomb when the game is on the line—and I can do it every time." As anyone who has played team sports knows, the common commitment and shared pain are emotionally important to the sense of being on the same team.

In the same way, few men would say what I have heard from many women: "It shouldn't matter if I leave at four o'clock to get the kids, or if I can't put in the 'face time,' as long as I'm getting my work done." While I personally would agree with that statement, it was clear that, in a subtle way, many of the men I spoke with wouldn't. Any man will say that it makes sense, logically. But emotionally they feel that such a person isn't really sharing the same commitment to the team.

> Few men would say what I have heard from many women: "It shouldn't matter if I leave at four o'clock as long as I'm getting my work done."

One software-development manager described it this way: "Results are important, but there is also something about a shared burden and feeling the pain together. If we're in the middle of a big project, and there is someone in the department who still has to leave at three p.m. every day to pick her kids up—but I know that from nine to midnight she's actually going to be intensively working and doing the stuff she was unable to do from three to six with the rest of the team, then I have no problem. I know she's feeling the same pain; she's just spreading it out over different hours. It isn't necessarily whether or not she has to leave early if we have agreed to that—but whether she's feeling the same pain."

Then he grimaced, and added, "But there's a problem even with that. It's really hard to show that you're feeling the same pain if you're not at the office. Anyone who works long hours gets really good at cutting through the baloney about whether the pain is really being shared. I had one female colleague who scooted out every day at five o'clock—which for us is really early. But then I'd get these croaking voice mails from her timed at one a.m. to prove how hard she was working from home. Okay, fine—but there was never any document in my inbox in the morning. So if she was working those hours, it didn't translate into results."

You show that you are fully invested in shared goals by a consistent willingness to sacrifice something of value (time with family, sleep, money) for the sake of achieving those goals. Men (and many women, for that matter) are constantly watching to see whether other workers seem fully "invested"—whether they intimately care about the same goals. Quite a few men mentioned the importance of loyalty. As one man put it, "The feeling that you can trust someone to be loyal is invaluable." But it took me awhile to realize that what they often meant by loyalty was, in actuality, being invested in and caring about the same goals.

And the primary signal to show how much someone cares seems to be whether they are willing to sacrifice something of value for it. Whenever there is extra work to be done, is the person willing to give up sleep, time with family, or those much-looked-forward-to tickets to the big game? In a partnership or an entrepreneurial venture, are they willing to spend their own money or put in some sweat equity instead of taking a regular salary? When they get their own work done, instead of heading out the door, are they willing to chip in and ask their boss or co-workers, "What can I do to help you so we can both get out of here before dinner?"

Now, clearly, this "willingness to sacrifice" dynamic may not be a healthy one. Some people end up feeling like they have no choice but to give up family time for the sake of demonstrating commitment to their job. As we'll discuss more in chapter 5, I love it when I see talented and committed women being a part of changing those unbalanced expectations.

THE ROAD TO UNDERSTANDING

Given that so many men feel this burden—and so many women don't recognize that it's there—it is likely that there will always be a certain degree of tension around this issue. Especially since we simply may not agree with men's expectations or, for that matter, with the "world will stop spinning" fear that sparks those expectations in the first place.

But regardless of whether we agree, it is vital to understand what signals we send our male colleagues, bosses, employees, and clients, simply because this concern is so overwhelmingly vital to them. Then, at least, we'll be able to make informed decisions in any given situation and respond with the sort of collegiality and understanding that will itself be proof to those watching that we really are "all in" with the team.

CHAPTER 4

"I Can't Handle It"

The Little Things That Drive Men Crazy

For just this one time in the book, I'm going to break my rule of only including quotes from men who seemed to genuinely care about women's advancement and relay a comment I overheard in a crowded airline club room. A fifty-something businessman was on a conference call on his cell phone, sitting a few feet from me, and I could hear everything he was saying. I ignored him as best I could until the topic of the call turned to a woman he worked with.

I overheard him say, "Yeah, but she just makes such a big deal of it if you bring something up. It just becomes too big of a fuss to manage." After listening a moment, he added, "I just can't handle it anymore. Better to not deal with it and maybe she'll find it difficult enough that she'll look elsewhere on her own."

I quietly pulled out my quote notebook, resisted the temptation to whack him upside the head with it, and began to record what he was saying. Because the irritation unfolding in front of me exemplified something I've heard from many men: All too often, it's the little things that most drive them crazy. Big-picture issues (like whether someone doesn't seem to share his fear that the world will stop spinning) will impact how a man perceives someone, but they don't necessarily irritate him. The little things, however, all too easily rub a man the wrong way, and over time they can add up to a significant negative impact.

Thankfully, because they are relatively minor issues, they are also relatively easy to address...as long as we're aware of them.

Undoubtedly there are dozens of little things that irritate men (and women, for that matter). In this chapter, I will cover three that I heard frequently and that seem most representative of this dynamic: when colleagues don't get to the point, when they overreact, or when they don't let things go. Let's look at each in turn.

"THEY DON'T GET TO THE POINT"

Speaking at a church women's event, I was amused when the women's ministry director recounted a favorite phrase that her boss, the pastor, used when he was in "business" mode: "Don't tell me about the pain; just show me the baby."

That pretty much sums up how men expect discussions in the working world to operate. As you saw in chapter 1, while they may listen to details, stories, and long recountings of Personal World, they don't expect to do so in the workplace. In the workplace, efficiency dominates and, men tell me, they have neither the natural wiring to process a lot of details nor the patience for them. As many men put it, "Give me the conclusion up front, and if I need more detail, I'll ask."

This is not likely to be a surprise; most women have probably heard this in their careers—and even from men at home. But I was surprised at the level of frustration or impatience men felt at seemingly "minor inconveniences" like having to wait for the end of a story to hear the conclusion, wading through unwanted details, or enduring unrelated conversation at the beginning of a meeting. The men I interviewed and surveyed helped me to understand the reasons why those nuisances are perceived so poorly. Let's tackle each of them briefly.

Men need to hear the conclusion up front

The way many of the men I interviewed described it, they prefer the conclusion or the bottom line up front because it helps them listen. Without it, they find it more difficult to absorb the information.

> *Men prefer the conclusion or the bottom line up front because it helps them listen.*

One executive explained,

There's something about a male brain that wants the end of the story so he knows why he's listening. He's already focused on one thing, and if he's switching to another he needs to know what it is. And if he knows, it actually helps him listen. It's comforting to him, versus when you wonder, "Where is she going with this?" There is an actual discomfort in not knowing.

For example, this morning one woman was describing something that happened with a client, and she was telling me this story, and I didn't know if she was going to end with, "So isn't that funny?" or "So we lost the account." Listening that way is hard and uncomfortable for a guy. If you can come in and make it immediately clear what you're talking about and how it relates to what he's doing, it will make a big difference. Men are much more patient with moving their focus when there is clarity.

Another executive tied this to men's relative difficulty with multitasking: "When you start a story, guys are trying to understand the relevance and context. And we really can't do that and listen well at the same time. So if he's wondering, 'Why are you telling me this?' he's not going to be hearing you properly."

On my survey, 60 percent of men agreed—and that percentage was higher the more senior the men were and the larger their company. Of executives in companies with more than $20 million in annual revenues, 70 percent said they feel like it is harder to listen and follow what someone is saying if they don't state the point up front.

If he needs more detail, he'll ask for it

In *Why Men Don't Listen and Women Can't Read Maps*, Barbara and Allan Pease nail the reason for men's frequent request for fewer details. "Women's brains are process-oriented *and they enjoy the process of communicating* [emphasis mine]. Men find this lack of structure and purpose very disconcerting."[1]

Every branch of science studying how men and women communicate has found that women tend to process externally (they think something through by talking it through), while men tend to process internally (while they are thinking it through, they often *can't* talk about it). In large measure, this is due to the differences in brain structure covered in other chapters.

To a man, however, the woman who is processing verbally may simply look scatterbrained. And it is all too easy for him to get exasperated. (*I can't follow this. Why is she wasting my time?*) As one man put it, "I'm impatient with people who make me have to work out what the heck they are talking about. You're making me work too hard to understand you."

Women presumably share the details because (as verbal processors) we instinctively assume that our listener similarly needs to hear our thought process to understand that we thought through all the permutations. Men, however, are used to processing internally and *not* hearing all those permutations—and they usually prefer not to.

One man advised, "Start with the end of the story, and work backward," sharing only a few details about how you got there. By doing that, he said, you are essentially putting both parties at the same starting point. And the man can ask for more details as needed going forward.

> *To a man, the woman who is processing verbally may simply look scatterbrained.*

Look at this representative comment from the vice president of human resources at a large technology company: "I think a man wants to know, 'What is the bottom line?' A woman wants to tell a story, and for a man, that is just a waste of time. If there is important context to be shared, then okay. But nine times out of ten, just start with the bottom line and if I want more, I will tell you."

He went on, "I do not need to know the whole story and the rest of the problem. I just need to know that for a $10 million budget, we look like we will be $500,000 off. Okay, start with that. Now I understand the problem, and I am definitely listening. Next, I need to understand why we're $500,000 off and how we got there. But do not start with how we got there. Start with the bottom line and then work backward. Get me on the same page with you. And then I may ask for more."

Now, there is one important caveat to this "If I need more details I will ask" rule: it appears limited primarily to a supervisor/subordinate relationship. As we'll see in later chapters, junior men and even peers may not feel comfortable admitting that they don't understand something or that they need additional details. But even the more junior men said that they need others to start with the bottom line and limit details to some degree, especially in response to a question.

One manager gave me an example of what that looks like: "I told a new female hire, 'It would help if you could first just answer the question that I have asked you. If you need to give me the additional information, fine, but first answer the question.' I guess no one had ever been willing to bring that up with her before. But she instantly got it, and I am really enjoying working with her now. There's not that frustration in the background."

To some men, verbal processing can even make the speaker look insecure. Randal, the CFO of a small New York media company, told me,

> I have several women who work in my department who seem to want to tell me their process so I can appreciate all the hard work that they did. But men assume that if you have got there, then you have done all of that. I also frankly think there is an insecurity that I am going to reject what they are saying if they don't give all the details; that I'm not going to give it enough weight.
>
> By contrast, there is another woman I work with closely who is really great about summarizing. She will say to me, "These are the options and this is what I think." That is very effective. It is sort of a hybrid approach; she can get out the details that she thinks are critical, but gives me the bottom line.

It is ironic that the detailed processing some men experience as frustrating and irrelevant can actually be a strength in women. One representative sales manager explained his annoyance with how his female staff turn what could be a ten-minute meeting ("Okay, what do you guys want to do? Good, let's do it") into a longer discussion about whether the process is right. But as he acknowledged, "Guys could go out of the ten-minute meeting and just completely botch the job because they did not spend enough time in analyzing the problem. There is benefit to be had from that additional deliberation. There is strength in how women handle things, but for men to understand it and perceive it that way is the issue."

Men tend to see small talk as irrelevant and wasteful

As women who tend not to see the same sort of strict separation between Personal and Work Worlds, we often find value in building relationships with co-workers through touching base or catching up on personal matters before getting down to business. The problem is that many men see such small talk as completely irrelevant to the business and as an exasperating way to squander limited time. And they largely have the same impression of discussions that are work related but have nothing to do with the purpose of that particular meeting.

When I asked the men on my survey if there were things they saw talented women do to undermine themselves with men, one answered, "This sounds terrible, but [it is] the chatting. All the mindless talking that seems to take up the first half of any conversation."

As Jeffery Tobias Halter, author of *Selling to Men, Selling to Women*, put it in a recent talk,

> As a rule of thumb, 80 percent of the time, men are transactional and women are relational. You can always tell transactional people from relational people by walking into a meeting and asking, "How was your weekend?" The relational person will tell you they went to the lake with their kids, and open up an opportunity for you to ask, "How many kids do you have?" And talk back and forth

for a few minutes. The transactional person will answer, "Fine." If they are the senior person in the meeting, that is your cue to avoid the relational talk at all costs. Otherwise, they'll think you are wasting their time.[2]

This is another area where women might legitimately perceive a business value in spending time on issues beyond the immediate work matter at hand. For example, in conference calls or in meetings, I personally am very transactional. I have little margin in my schedule, so I can easily get impatient with time spent on conversation that I view as extraneous.

Yet all the women who work for me are very relationship oriented, and when we start our biweekly morning-long staff meetings, it's common for us to spend a few minutes catching up on kids or weekend plans or a husband's job situation. This was torture for me, and I kept trying to eliminate it, until my staff director took me aside and told me bluntly, "Your team needs this. We are scattered doing all these different things. To continue to enjoy our jobs and enjoy working together, we need this time together to hear what is going on in each other's lives. And we need to hear what is going on in yours. Take the extra five minutes and tell us about what happened at your event last weekend. That is part of what keeps us cohesive and motivated."

Once I was willing to relax a bit and not try to hurry to get down to business, I saw that my staff director was correct. I imagine that many women have had that conversation with a male boss (and some female bosses, for that matter), who has probably seen the same results. Yet until you attempt to address it directly, and in terms of value, it is important to be aware how negatively the "extra conversation" is likely to be perceived by many of your male colleagues.

Two-thirds of men (including Christian men) on the survey

said that if a female colleague came into their office to talk one on one about issues beyond the workplace, they either were "likely to have" or "may have" the feeling: *I should discuss it with her, to show that I care...but privately, I'd really rather not, because I fear I'll get sucked into a personal conversation, and I just don't have time for that here.*

Whether the topic under discussion is personal or is related to other work issues, men appear likely to view the person who doesn't immediately get down to the business at hand as not only nonbusinesslike, but high maintenance.

The media company CFO, Randal, provided an example that he viewed as "fairly common," especially in a Christian-led environment such as his, where some employees expected more of a listening ear:

> We had just acquired a company, and I was running an integration project with two team leaders, one woman and one man. With the woman, I had to spend an amount of time just sitting and listening to her, and that was really frustrating. She would come to me, explaining her issues with her team that I had assigned to her.... I honestly didn't think the issues were that big of a deal, but I had to deal with it.
>
> But with the male team leader, I had actually given him a much more difficult team, with a bunch of different work styles he was going to have to blend. He had a bunch of what we would call the old-timers in this field, late forties and fifties, who were resisting doing things the new way. And I gave them this thirty-something guy as a leader.
>
> And he has this whole bunch of dynamics that was far beyond what he could envision, but he would come to

me and simply tell me what the problem was and how he had solved it or was planning on solving it. He would briefly fill me in, or bounce something off me to make sure I was okay with what he was planning to do. And that was just so much better, honestly. He was a much more low-maintenance employee than she was. I found her a high-maintenance employee. That is not to discount how talented she was and how hard she tried, how much time she invested in doing her role. But if I had to choose who I would rather work with, I would work with the guy.

"THEY OVERREACT"

As we saw in earlier chapters (and in the story at the beginning of this one), men place a high value on being able to address concerns or offer a criticism directly, without worrying about how someone is going to react. The men I interviewed told me that once they started having to worry about that, it was hard not to let their wariness color all of their interactions with that person.

> *Men place a high value on being able to address concerns or offer a criticism directly, without worrying about how someone is going to react.*

A man on the survey provided this example:

My co-worker actually got emotional in a meeting when asked to explain her testing technique. Instead of answering the question as a matter of informing the guy, she assumed he was questioning her skills. I ended up having to rephrase the question for her to understand it from a nonconfrontational viewpoint. Now to this day a lot of the programmers are wary of getting her involved in discussions and assume she can't handle pressure well.

When men I surveyed brought up the "don't overreact" issue as an example of how women sabotage the way men perceive them, remarks ranged from, "Get overly upset when someone disagrees with them" to "Take suggestions of how to improve things too personally" to "Become overly heated during a simple exchange of ideas."

As you can tell, the concern about "overreacting" is inextricably linked to what we've seen in earlier chapters about not taking things personally and not getting emotional. As discussed in those chapters, managing how we are perceived often requires a purposeful edit of our reactions before we let anything show.

And that "edit" might be especially useful to muster when it is a male colleague who is overreacting. Geoff, the Fortune 500 CMO said,

> Women at senior levels have to understand that sometimes, men overreact big too. And women can't overreact to their overreaction. Remember, he'll be done in ten minutes and won't think about it the rest of the day. Some men will even overreact for effect. Not long ago our CEO got mad in a senior meeting. He never swears, but he used the F-bomb with a direct report, to make a point. The guy the anger was directed at didn't overreact, didn't take it to HR, and I saw them having lunch three days later. So if men overreact they don't mean it forever.

And that leads to the third issue commonly mentioned by the men I interviewed.

"THEY JUST WON'T LET IT GO"

This is one of the "little things" that men found the most inexplicable: the tendency of a worker (most frequently a woman) to hold a grudge. Because men tend to think of Work World as a place where you essentially become your position and take your personal self out of it, men rarely show personal animus as the result of a workplace conflict. And they are not only irritated but alarmed when women do, viewing an unwillingness (or inability) to "let it go" as a character flaw and potential threat to the business.

When asked what a talented woman might do to undermine her perception with men, one survey taker answered, "Two women may get into an emotional confrontation and may not forgive each other for it. The aftereffect is that a man that works between their two departments will have to suffer the hostility and bitterness between the two women, making them seem less desirable employees to upper management."

A business owner I was speaking with brought this subject up, describing such a situation as a "personal conflict." His colleague jumped in: "Actually, it may look personal. But the man's mind moves it immediately out of the personal category to the business category. The man isn't looking at two women having a catfight. He's looking at a threat to the business. That's the impact it has."

The business owner added, "It is the same threat if a man is doing it. Our chief technology officer didn't let things go, and it was viewed as a serious character flaw, and we had to fire him."

I asked the men on the survey a series of questions about their perceptions in this area, and their answers were stark. On average, three out of four men looked quite negatively at someone who did not let a conflict go, perceiving that as a big problem for the company and the individual's career. Rather than summarize these perceptions, I'm going to include the full list here. In the question,

I was not specifically asking about women, but about anyone who expressed annoyance with another co-worker over time.

Consider times in your working life when you have seen two co-workers have a work-related conflict and then begin to express annoyance with each other over time. Did you have any of the following perceptions about the situation and those co-workers? (Choose one answer on each row below.)

	I DID THINK THAT	I DID NOT THINK THAT
a. Getting personal in the workplace is not appropriate	77%	23%
b. This is wasting time and hurting the organization's efficiency	82	18
c. It makes me think they are choosing to not set this aside	73	27
d. It makes me think that they are incapable of setting this aside	61	39
e. Handling things this way could limit their professional opportunities	79	21
f. Whatever else I think about it, I do not want to get dragged in	74	26
g. It won't negatively impact the business, so it's fine if they process things this way	19	81

Elsewhere on the survey, 49 percent of men said that "if people become annoyed with each other, it is important for them to be able to express it openly, in their own way." Yet I believe this is an example of men who were trying to be sensitive and politically correct, but didn't actually believe what they were saying. *Fully 80 percent of those same men* said that continuing to express annoyance after a conflict (which presumably was an example of someone "expressing it openly, in their own way") wasted time and hurt efficiency. Even more telling, 79 percent of those men essentially felt that although the person "should" be able to express themselves openly, actually doing so would hurt the person's career.

> Men view an unwillingness (or inability) to "let it go" as a character flaw and potential threat to the business.

Although the men were straightforward about the harm of not letting something go after a conflict, the men were significantly

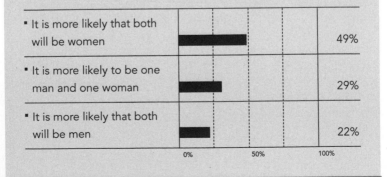

Now, this is a sensitive question, but your anonymous input will be helpful. In the type of scenario you recollected for the [previous question], in your experience what is more likely to be the gender of those expressing annoyance? (Choose one answer.)

▪ It is more likely that both will be women	49%
▪ It is more likely to be one man and one woman	29%
▪ It is more likely that both will be men	22%

0%   50%   100%

more cautious when I asked whether that was more likely with men or women.

In my personal interviews, nearly all the men I spoke with said that, realistically, such a two-sided scenario of continued annoyance was primarily observed among two female colleagues. While only half of the men on the survey put it that way, nearly eight in ten men did indicate that when those situations occurred, a woman would be involved. It was much less likely to be seen among two men.

Ironically, although the male survey takers were cautious about naming women as those most often observed in that behavior, the control group of female survey takers wasn't. Among the female survey takers, fully 73 percent said both parties would likely be women, 20 percent said it would be one man and one woman, and just 7 percent said it was likely for both parties to be men.

In one interview, Dominic, the owner of a fifty-person manufacturing company, recounted the frustration that arose when he watched a male and female director get into spats over e-mail. "For crying out loud," he remembered thinking, "you're twenty feet apart; stop using e-mail where you misinterpret and misread things. Just get out of your chair and go down and talk to this person. You know, I think I've spent more time wearing my striped shirt and referee hat once I got these women in there, in director roles."

I then pointed out, "But this can't really be just something women specifically need to know, if men do it too."

Dominic paused and chose his words carefully:

I will say this: When I have two men in key roles, I don't have those conversations. Ever. I don't mean to suggest that when it was one man and one woman that it was all the woman's fault. I'm just saying there was more noise that I had to deal with when a woman was involved. I was looking forward to hiring women, and I will do it again. A woman can be extremely productive in our particular field. But to be frank with you, there just are things that you deal with, with women, that you don't usually deal with, with guys.

And unfortunately, there are some ramifications for women that go beyond simple alarm or annoyance, and into a sense of uncertainty that could actually damage a working relationship. Cole, the executive search leader quoted in previous chapters, put it this way:

> I think men know that they can engage in this significant work-related conflict and generally not carry emotional baggage away from it. But men fear that if they engage in the similar level of intense conflict with a woman, that there will be emotional baggage that is carried away that will come back negatively in the future whether as resentment or as retaliation or revenge. They begin to be concerned that there will be an occasion all of a sudden, three weeks later in a meeting, where she will seize the opportunity to take a dig, thinking that this is a chance to even the score for something the guy thought was just a business conflict.
>
> What happens then is that the guy is unwilling to engage in the same level of business conflict because the future repercussions are not entirely predictable. And over time, the consequences of that will actually go deep for the woman, and for the company. Because if he's not willing to engage her, then he has to try to find ways to bypass her. And eventually the woman is marginalized or the business doesn't function properly.

So if men seem a bit more able and willing than women to let things go—why? Why is this something that men don't seem to struggle with as much?

A MAN'S BRAIN WIRING MAKES MANAGING EMOTIONAL CONFLICT MORE EXHAUSTING—AND MAKES "LETTING THINGS GO" MUCH EASIER

As you saw in chapter 2, the male brain simply isn't wired to process emotions or interpersonal conflicts as easily—which makes it actively unpleasant to hold on to things, or deal with those who do. So it is often more comfortable for them to ignore, avoid, or compartmentalize out those emotional and personality issues to begin with. By contrast, a large part of the tendency to hold on to something seems to be an unconscious response to the multitasking, noncompartmentalized nature of the female brain. Our research for *For Men Only* found that 81 percent of women have difficulty closing "mental windows" on issues that are bothering them. A concern tends to pop back up until whatever caused the concern is resolved.

My husband, Jeff, who coauthored and researched *For Men Only* with me, provided a helpful perspective on how differently the compartmentalized male brain handles things:

> As guys we tend not to talk about interpersonal conflicts to others. We clam up. If a guy is actually talking about it, that means it is such a big deal that he hasn't been able to stuff it, he hasn't been able to compartmentalize it. So if I see a woman talking about these conflicts, I assume this is such a huge thing for her that she can't *not* talk about it. But it's really just a difference in perception. I look at the conflict and think, *Why is this such a huge deal for her?* when she may actually be experiencing the exact same feeling as I am, but just handling it differently.
>
> The problem is that to a guy, her reaction could look like a lack of self-control, or as if she could be letting this go but is choosing not to. Or that she's making something a big deal that shouldn't be a big deal. And unfortunately, any of those could be seen as a weakness.

A MAN TENDS TO INTERPRET LETTING THINGS GO AS A SIGN OF STRENGTH—AND NOT DOING SO AS A SIGN OF WEAKNESS
Men's need to "let it go" appears to be heightened by social pressure. An executive of a multinational company described how men handle such concerns:

> Among men, there is something unmanly about remembering something. It shows a weakness in yourself. It shows that your armor was chinked in that conflict and you remember it. Why would you want to bring something up that happened two weeks ago or two months ago or two years ago? You forget it because you move on. And you move on because to do otherwise shows weakness. It is like: You fall, skin your knee, shake it off, and move on. In business, it happened, it is done, there's no need to deliberate about it, forget it. So you go have a few drinks and everything is done.

"Among men, there is something unmanly about remembering something. You move on because to do otherwise shows weakness."

A MAN'S PREFERRED SOLUTION IS TO ADDRESS A CONCERN DIRECTLY, THEN DROP IT
In men's minds, the solution is to address an issue of concern directly and then simply not bring it up again. Three out of four men on the survey chose that approach. Another 22 percent said one should "stuff" the feeling of annoyance or should never have allowed oneself those feelings to begin with. Only 3 percent of men said it was acceptable to continue to express feelings of annoyance and let the situation naturally run its course.

Of course, the men's preferred solution isn't always easy for us to put into effect. We naturally wonder, *How can a woman address something from the past that truly needs to be addressed for a business purpose, without being perceived poorly?* I put that question to the multinational executive I quoted earlier:

ME: Suppose that a woman is ticked off that a colleague did something he shouldn't have. And the next year the guy is up for promotion and she feels the issue will affect the business. How can she raise it?

HIM: I would want to see that there is a sterile analysis of it. It is not an emotional analysis of it. So her first problem is that people saw her getting ticked about the situation to begin with. If she hadn't done that, her analysis a year later would seem a lot more credible. You need to show that when you look at it, you are looking at it through the lens of "We have these pros and these cons. This guy has delivered these results but there is this problem from last year." You can enumerate the problems but you look at it rationally in a detached fashion, not emotionally. You are not getting bent about it.

Another man responded with a different example:

We do have a problem with someone who seems to be keeping the pot stirred. But we're not robots. If I have had a business problem with someone, I'll move past it, but it doesn't mean that the problem is erased from my memory bank. We're not necessarily starting from a blank slate on the next deal. I'm just not going to let it impinge on what I'm doing today. It's a choice I have to make.

Letting it go doesn't mean that I've forgotten it and

expect a problematic colleague to be different next time. If I've found him to be untrustworthy once, I assume he'll still be untrustworthy next time. So I won't go back to him next time with a similar thing. But on everything else, we may not like each other or see eye to eye, but we can put the personal stuff aside and focus on what needs to be done.

> "Letting it go doesn't mean that I've forgotten it and expect a problematic colleague to be different next time."

PERSONAL STUFF ASIDE, NOW WHAT?

As I've been describing the little things some co-workers do that drive men crazy, you may have been thinking that men are simply unrealistic in what they expect from a diverse workplace. Or you might have been thinking, *Well, of course that behavior drives them crazy—it drives me crazy too!* Whatever your response, I hope you don't miss the good news: where needed, small changes of pattern can lead to big impacts in perception.

The key for us is to learn to read our male colleagues and understand when an approach that comes naturally for us may be causing conflict, stress, or discomfort for them. We can then decide where a change might smooth the way for both of us.

The men I interviewed clearly felt that when professional women were willing to do that, it not only helped eliminate discomfort, but it also freed up the men to see the specific strengths that the female colleague had been bringing to the situation the entire time—strengths that might otherwise have been missed.

Here's just one of many encouraging examples that I heard.

This one came as I was talking with a business owner about the "letting it go" issue, but the principle applies to all:

> For companies to be successful, if you make mistakes, you learn from them and you move forward. I think men do keep scorecards, and they essentially expect that everyone else will too. But they expect it to be in a detailed and organized way, not an emotional way. They expect it to be solely on issues affecting the business.
>
> Men keep up with those things, but they use their scorecard to make specific work-related decisions going forward. Now, if a woman makes it clear that that is what she is doing, the perception will completely change. Women can sometimes be more observant. If she shows that she has observed something and she is taking her personal feelings out of it and putting it purely in a business-scorecard context, that would be immensely valuable. Instead of being looked at as a gossip or as lacking maturity, she will be seen as someone who has excellent corporate intelligence and who uses it well.

CHAPTER 5

"Suck It Up"

Getting It Done No Matter What

When boys play even an informal game of football or basketball, they usually play hard. They may be on the grass of the city park or a half court by the old fire station, but they play like it's televised on ESPN. Inevitably someone gets hurt—a face is badly scratched, a nose is bloodied, a kid gets the wind knocked out of him.

When that happens, are the others likely to crowd around, asking, "You okay?" Well, if the boy is unconscious or coughing up blood, maybe. Otherwise, the expectation of everyone—including the wounded competitor—is the same: Suck it up and keep playing. No excuses, no complaining, no asking for special consideration.

Men hold the same expectation in the workplace. In my interviews, sports-related analogies came up over and over again, and the "suck it up" mind-set clearly affected everything from how men (and some women) viewed alternative working arrangements like flextime, to what they expected of any good employee. Interestingly, of all the insights men shared for this book, several of the points in this chapter were also those that men felt most uncomfortable voicing directly.

And you, in turn, may feel uncomfortable hearing such honesty. I was. Unspoken male expectations in this area are not only surprising but often hit a nerve for women today. I did observe a few differences between men in general and men with a Christian mind-set or in Christian environments. But regardless, the "suck it up" mind-set is pervasive in the workplace and vital for us to understand. In fact, this is one of the clearest examples of an area where we may disagree with a male viewpoint and yet find it invaluable to know what it is. Once we have this inside knowledge, we can make informed decisions and set the expectations that are right for us, while knowing exactly how our choices will be perceived.

Let's look at what feeds this mind-set and the expectations that come with it.

COWBOY UP, MAN UP, SUCK IT UP: WHAT THEY MEAN

To understand the "suck it up" mind-set at work (and how people are perceived because of it), we have to understand just how much men see the world in terms of competition. For most men, everyday life is framed by "you versus me," "us versus them," and—even if there's no other competition—"me versus myself." All the expectations in this chapter would be merely academic if not for the fact that workers do in fact compete for compensation, promotion, and prestige. Even men in collaborative, team-oriented jobs see themselves in competition to get ahead, not just with that other company across town, but with members of their team.

This is why men seem so highly attuned to how hard everyone plays the game—and whether everyone is playing by the same rules. (This is not, as in chapter 1, about the big-picture "rules of the workplace," but about whether a man sees all colleagues having a level playing field for the competition between them.)

This mind-set lends itself to four very common male expectations.

Expectation 1: You don't let obstacles stop you from getting the job done

From a player's earliest age, the expectations of coaches, teammates, and his or her own internal drive create the most fundamental rule of any competitive endeavor: if you have accepted a particular spot on the team, you don't let obstacles keep you from getting the job done.

In a man's mind, business endeavors work the same way. Just as any competitive sports player (man or woman) expects banged-up teammates to get themselves off the ground and back into the game, men expect colleagues to push themselves to get the job done even when flu, difficult clients, technology glitches, personal problems, or a sick child intervene.

The CFO of a Fortune 500 manufacturer said men see things this way:

> I played soccer all my life, and if your teammate has a hard collision, you may encourage him with a slap on the back, but you say, "Let's get it done." Certainly when you take a hit, you know you'd better get up and keep playing. If you're really hurt, you take yourself out of the game. If someone doesn't take himself out, you don't expect to see him limping along at half speed. You get your act together or get off the field. Men naturally expect that mind-set from other men—and from women as well.

Although this comment may seem cold, the CFO was, in fact, a sensitive individual. As I saw in many of my interviews, the "suck it up" mentality exists even when a man is caring and sympathetic. The reason, according to one engineer:

You *expect* to have to prove yourself every day. It's not just about competence but your ability to get the job done *that day*. When we're in the business equivalent of third and ten, and the game is on the line, I'm going to put in the person who has proved he or she can get it done, period. I'm simply not going to put in someone who has shown that they can't always be 100 percent. If you're at all aware of how business works, there is no way that should be controversial or a surprise.

> "When we're in the business equivalent of third and ten, and the game is on the line, I'm going to put in the person who has proved he or she can get it done, period."

Over and again, men emphasized that it's not gender but performance that makes the difference. One man said, "I don't care if the person on the line is a man, woman, or little green-eyed monster. They get my respect when they prove themselves." So, in a man's eyes, what constitutes "proving yourself" and thus getting that respect? There are several key factors that I heard over and over again.

You push through obstacles. A man respects a person whom he sees as pushing through obstacles to get something accomplished. And the willingness and ability to do so is a large part of what makes the man consider someone a reliable or key player instead of a marginal one. At the same time, the colleague who pushes through does not necessarily receive applause or appreciation. Why? To other men, the colleague is merely adhering to the rules of Work World and doing what's expected. Conversely, colleagues who don't meet that expectation—who let those obstacles "defeat" them or prevent the job from getting done well—lose respect. Privately, a man will question their dependability, mentally relegating them to bench players.

On my national survey, one man said women may unintentionally undermine themselves "when [they have] major responsibilities and [don't] show up because of minor physical or emotional problems [or don't] work through obstacles to do her job."

I read that quote to a male colleague, who shook his head and said, "Who gets to say that a physical or emotional problem is 'minor'? Unfortunately for women, men often don't understand many of the issues women deal with, and so often view those issues as minor when they're not."

However, the reality is that even when a man views an outside issue as important, it is still (under this view) supposed to take a backseat to the person's workplace responsibilities. While Christian environments tend to prioritize family as most important and extend more grace, workers still are expected to show a willingness to push through even big obstacles to meet goals. As one person on my test survey advised, "Be cautious how [you] bring discussions of children's issues into the workplace. We all love our children! We all must also make provisions for them when they're sick or need help at school.... But [giving] 100 percent while at work is the rule."

If necessary, you right-size your expectations. When a worker is actually hindered by obstacles that can't be worked through, that person will retain (or even increase) a man's respect by adjusting expectations away from trying to be a first-string player for a time. If the worker acknowledges that the obstacles will hinder the team's chances of winning (for example, landing the deal or getting the report in on time), he or she may be able to carve out a less demanding role for a period of time. Such a person is far more likely to get respect than the one who continually insists they can get it done, then doesn't.

In a private meeting with a group of managers at a huge household-name company, the female hiring director described a talk she has to have with "many more" up-and-coming women than men. She said women with children who rise through the ranks often come to a crisis point. She takes them aside and tells them, "You're going to have to choose whether to prioritize your family or your career right now. By trying to prioritize both, you're doing neither well. Your work is suffering. If you want to keep doing this job well and rising in your career right now, your family has to take a backseat. If you want to prioritize your family, you need to adjust your job track. You have to make whatever choice is right for you—but very soon now, you're going to have to make a choice."

Hearing that story, one ambitious female friend of mine who does not have children said indignantly, "How has that company not been sued? How can she get away with that?"

> "You have to make whatever choice is right for you—but you're going to have to make a choice."

A more senior woman, listening in, said, "Because it's true! She's giving a woman the chance to be purposeful about a decision, before the decision is made for her by being fired or humiliated within the organization, or before her family falls apart. It's better for women if we're honest and realistic with ourselves—and each other." I might also point out it's better for men too! It's just that men are more likely to know that these expectations are there.

You signal day-to-day commitment. Since men expect colleagues or subordinates to get their act together when they encounter obstacles, they certainly expect them to demonstrate complete commitment during normal times—and to never signal a lack of commitment.

Men I interviewed confessed that when they had seen someone signal a lack of commitment, that person was, in their experience, much more likely to be a woman. The men would often hasten to say, "But I don't think this is a gender issue" and "I'm sure men do this too." Yet every single time I asked, "Can you give me an example of when you've seen a man do this?" the answer was always, "Well…no."

Men may have simply learned how to hide any apathy or difficulty, instead of broadcasting it. Brad, a junior partner at a large national law firm, described it this way:

> I see sometimes where a woman comes out of law school and has no intention of staying to become a partner. Without intending to, she broadcasts an attitude of "I'm only going to be here a few years; at some point I'm going to ramp down my schedule when I have kids." Okay, more power to her; that's her choice. But then you see this winding down of mental commitment to the job. Now, I'm thankful we live in an age where a woman can be valued for choosing to be a mom. My wife is making that choice. But maybe because there isn't a stigma anymore, sometimes a younger woman doesn't think she needs to make people think she is mentally invested. So she doesn't spend the time you would expect, or leaves a project for a more senior person to correct and finish, or doesn't go the extra mile to figure out something technical. Look, I don't love learning certain technicalities of Delaware tax law. But it's a pill I know I need to swallow because I'm going to be doing this as my career, to provide for my family, and so I need to build my skill set. If I saw a man not taking the extra time, I would think, *He's checking out and about to move to another job.*

Expectation 2: You don't complain

Just as men believe you suck it up and get the job done despite obstacles, they also believe you don't draw attention to or complain about those obstacles. That means dealing with all hindrances with aplomb, pushing through them by working harder, and not drawing attention to how much you have to deal with. Doing otherwise is akin to crying on the football field, "Coach, that big, mean linebacker hit me too hard!" Even when there's something worth complaining about, it just isn't done.

And what is seen as complaining is far more than merely saying, "This is unfair." For example, blaming institutional bias (including gender bias) for anything was seen as whiny. An investment company executive said,

> If the men at my company get annoyed that the higher-ups seem biased in favor of promoting folks from Ivy League business schools, the other guys say, "Well, okay, then I have to suck it up, work harder, and prove I can compete." If you complain instead, then you are seen as self-condemning, deficient, not capable of winning on your own merits, positioning yourself as a victim. Guys think, *What guy with testosterone in his body would go out there claiming to be a victim?* And they expect any woman who is serious will handle things the same way.

What I found fascinating is that he and others viewed complaining as "claiming to be a victim," which undermines how confident that person is perceived to be in their skills and abilities.

Belaboring your load or hours is akin to complaining. Even if you have to work harder, the men advised, don't act like it. In one focus group, a female management consultant told of a former colleague who supported her husband through cancer treatments by day and had to work late each night—and regularly mentioned it. Many associates were initially sympathetic but eventually grew frustrated. One man in the focus group said, "She did what was needed, but complained. Either don't do it—or do it and don't complain! If it happens too often, that person will be mentally sidelined."

Now, in my previous hometown of New York City, people put in insane hours at work and gained a sick sort of satisfaction and kudos from laboring longer than anyone else. In order to not brag directly ("I was working on the Becker merger until 2:00 a.m."), employees would come up with creative ways to send the message: the e-mail or voice mail sent to the boss at 1:14 a.m. was a well-worked strategy. Given the pressure to work around the clock, a savvy worker often resorted to the *appearance* of face time in order to sneak out "early" at 9:00 p.m., leaving the office lights on and a suit coat visibly draped across the back of his or her chair. Or my personal favorite: Calling into the office at midnight to page themselves so that "Bill Smith, you have a call on line three" would resound through the building for everyone else to hear. I'm certainly not advocating such pathological behavior, but it does illustrate just how out of whack the "suck it up" expectations can get.

One behavior that also strikes men as whiny is getting agitated or stressed about minor issues instead of dealing with them in a calm and deliberate way. Their advice? One survey taker advised: "Don't sweat the small stuff. Once a woman is known as a complainer, management will walk the other way when they see her."

Here's another vital point: perhaps unfairly, men think talking about personal issues at work (read: complaining) means work is being negatively affected. A female senior vice president at a major corporation described this advice received by a female peer who was going through a divorce: "Don't let anyone at work know, or the guys may think you are going to fall apart." This may seem so cold, but I repeatedly heard men raise this as an issue. And frankly, this misperception may arise even more in ministry work environments, where people are more used to hearing about one another's lives.

Now, men obviously have personal issues to deal with too. "The problem," one of my female advisors observed, "is that it is more obvious with women because women tend to be more verbal."

Expectation 3: You don't ask for help or explanation

In the basketball movie *Hoosiers*, Gene Hackman plays the new coach of the tiny 1952 rural Indiana high school basketball team that eventually wins the state championship. When the season starts, though, he institutes a completely new style of play with no explanations as to why. Where previous coaches encouraged players to shoot for the basket whenever they had an opening ("If you don't shoot, you can't score!"), the new coach insists they not try for a basket until they pass at least four times. The team starts clumsily and loses its opening games. Frustrated, one player defies the coach and begins making baskets without passing. He is yanked from the game by the irate coach, leaving just four players against the other team's five.

In the locker room after the game, the coach tells the team, "For those of you on the floor at the end, I'm proud of you. You played your guts out. I'm only going to say this one time... Think about whether you want to be on this team or not, under the following condition: What I say when it comes to this basketball team *is the law absolutely and with no discussion!*"

After the movie, I asked my husband, Jeff, "Why didn't the coach just tell them why he insisted on four passes before shooting? If he had just explained the reason for the rule, the players would have understood, been on board, and wouldn't have gotten frustrated!"

Jeff, who played every conceivable sport in high school, replied, "In sports, guys generally don't ask why, and I'm guessing girls who play competitive sports don't either. The coach is the law. He doesn't have to explain himself. That doesn't mean all questions are off-limits. There is a way to ask without seeming to question the coach, but especially when you're under time pressure, you're expected to just do what he says. Guys tend to think that if you don't understand why you're doing something, you should be able to figure it out on your own."

> "Guys think that if you don't understand why you're doing something, you should be able to figure it out on your own."

Many men I talked to pointed out ways this expectation transfers to the workplace.

What the boss says is the law. Men have been trained through sports, the classroom, Boy Scouts, the military, and the business world to work within a top-down hierarchy. Most men feel comfortable with that system, as everyone knows his or her place. Thus, employees may either love or resent their supervisor, but while that person is the boss, what he or she says goes. Anyone who doesn't get that is viewed as naive about the most basic rules at work.

As one manager said, "A lot of guys grow up learning that what the coach says is to be followed absolutely; you don't question it. We tend to view the edicts of the boss the same way. The boss says, 'Jump,' and your job is to ask, 'How high?' If the boss gives a task on deadline that you don't quite understand, you jump to get started anyway and think, *I have no idea what I'm doing, but I'll figure it out.*"

You figure it out on your own. Men will go out of their way to avoid asking for help. One businessman explained, "Asking means they couldn't figure it out on their own. So if they see a colleague asking for help or asking, 'What is the point behind this?' they automatically assume that person can't do it, can't figure it out."

This one factor affects working women far more than we realize, since women often have a natural desire to help others and aren't as reluctant to ask for help, whether that means stopping the car to ask for directions or popping into the boss's office to ask for more explanation on how to create the new budget report. For women, asking questions often seems the quickest and most efficient route to the answer; it certainly doesn't carry the stigma that "I can't figure this out on my own."

Many men acknowledged the downside to that mind-set. One senior manager said, "Men will definitely lean toward, 'You suck it up and do what you need to do,' and may even do it incorrectly instead of sharing problems or figuring out whether there's a better way to do it. Just put me in a cave and let me figure out how to do it. Men will do that often. I'm not sure that women will."

On a deadline, don't waste time looking for a better way. Not surprisingly, if the situation is time sensitive, men said they are more exasperated if someone wants to take time to ask, "Is there a better way of doing this?" Their instinct is to dive in and get started, and they may be annoyed or frustrated by our "need" to ask those extra questions.

Personally, I have a huge pet peeve against racing ahead with what seems like a half-baked process when a little extra front-end thought could dramatically improve things and save much time down the road. Why do so many men view it otherwise? I asked a man I'll call Harold, a managing partner of a Big Four accounting firm. Harold said,

> It depends on the perceived crisis by the manager. If someone says, "It has to get done right away," men want to see action steps immediately. If they see hesitation, they think that person can't do it. Men want, "We're in an emergency room, we need triage right away," not, "Let's get seven doctors in here and have a conference." But in reality, even with the large, urgent problems, 80 percent of the solution is defining what the problem is. Over the years I've seen a woman can be more effective at helping

define the problem because they are instinctively more willing to take the extra time to do so. Unfortunately, a man may view that as "they can't do it on their own."

Female executives I spoke with had seen this. One woman in a focus group said, "If some men didn't see a flurry of activity, they wrongly concluded I hadn't prioritized or wasn't taking action."

> *"If the men I worked with didn't see a flurry of activity, they wrongly concluded I hadn't prioritized or wasn't taking action."*

The problem is, women often sense that if we charge ahead in the face of unresolved concern, "There may," as one female consultant put it, "be a big price to pay." Harold suggested women proactively counter negative male concerns about a more measured approach:

Don't state your concern or question first. Instead, say, "I know a, b, and c are the steps we would normally take to handle this." You're demonstrating, "I know exactly what to do and could do it right now." Then state your concern. The guy will think, "She knows what to do, so there's a reason we should ask these questions first." Doing it in a different order totally changes the perception.

Expectation 4: You don't ask for different standards unless you are willing to adjust your expectations

This is a very sensitive topic. And for some women, it may be difficult to hear. But it is essential for anyone who feels torn between work and home-life responsibilities.

In the minds of men (and many women), the need for everyone

to play the game by the same rules is one of the most basic laws of the competitive working world. So even the most compassionate, accommodating men I spoke with shared the conviction that one simply does not ask for different standards, such as fewer working hours or a more flexible schedule, unless one also adjusts one's expectations to match those different standards.

The problem, they said, is that while most men seem to understand this "rule" and perceive when a boundary had been crossed, some women do not. In nearly every interview about this, men raised examples of women (usually, those with family responsibilities) appearing to expect equal treatment while asking for unequal standards. For example, being less available than other consultants to work nights and weekends, yet expecting the same opportunity to be included on the most exciting or lucrative deals, or being upset if they weren't.

Most of the examples were about working moms in demanding jobs, torn between the requirements of their work and their children. Men did not have the same perception about women who didn't have children and didn't have the same balancing act. Indeed, many childless women had the same perceptions as men. This was also observed less frequently in ministry work environments, where working moms seemed more likely to voluntarily step back from long-hour jobs (or, at times, felt more pressure to do so).

Almost every man I interviewed felt he could not openly address this dynamic without being misunderstood. One of my first in-depth business interviews was with a friend from my New York days, now a partner in a major consulting firm, whom I'll call Wes. Wes is a good guy and a sensitive manager. I figured he would give me a fair-minded but honest reaction about how a talented woman might create frustration among her male colleagues, in a way a talented man might not. I was surprised when he asked me to turn off my tape recorder before answering. The resulting discussion was long and challenging, but it was very representative of what I heard from dozens of other men.

WES, A PARTNER IN A MAJOR CONSULTING FIRM

There is a very common pet peeve that I've seen. We work hard here, right? We have big deals that come in at the last minute, sometimes need to pull all-nighters when we're trying to land or finish a project, and we need 100 percent effort from everyone. Now you know that I'm a family guy [Wes gestured to a picture of his wife and kids], but when the work comes in, you gotta do what you gotta do.

The problem is that expectations don't seem even. I've been working hard to get female associates hired here, and get them in on the good deals, but it's just a reality that if they have kids, they are more likely the ones who have to be home at a certain hour. Now, you know me—I personally think family has to take priority. If one of my female associates has a kid who's sick and she's got to leave, I want her to be able to do what she's gotta do. I don't want to make her feel guilty. If one of my daughters was sick, I would want my wife's boss to be generous about letting her run to the pediatrician.

But the reality is, that puts the rest of us in a bad spot. Someone is going to have to work double time to get that person's work done. No one ever, ever talks about this, but everyone—men and women—knows it's rarely a man who has to ask someone else to cover his work because of family obligations. We're okay with that, but there are consequences.

This just happened yesterday. A big deal finally crystallized yesterday afternoon, but one of my female associates had to leave as usual at six o'clock to pick up her son. My colleagues Steve and Jack were here at eleven o'clock at night, away from their own families, getting a deal memo put together without her help. And that's okay, because we want to be supportive and would want the same thing for our wives. [Wes leaned forward.] *But when it comes time to make partner, let's not pretend things are really equal.* That is what really, really irks men—and some women—around here.

We've got some incredibly smart, competent female associates. And some of them will bust their tail at midnight to get it done. But some others, usually the ones with families, simply can't. But they expect to be making partner, right along with Steve and Jack, who have been here twelve years but working far longer hours. And sometimes they do, honestly, because we're trying to increase our ratio of female partners, or even because we could be hit with a discrimination suit. But can you imagine what that says to Steve and Jack? They've sacrificed their time with their own families, after all. Women want equal treatment, but what Steve and Jack would probably be dying to say is, "Let's not pretend that things really were equal." Men can't really talk about it because they'd look like heels. But, privately, it's a very big frustration.

Wes's concern was echoed on our survey. Even when considering a fairly benign, common situation where two team members added great value but worked from home on Fridays, and due to family obligations weren't as able to stay late at the office during the week or on weekends, 57 percent of full-time men said the workload simply wasn't the same.

I found it heartening that more than four in ten men did view the two family-oriented workers as exactly the same, and saw that as good news for women who balance difficult work-life choices every day. That percentage probably signals the positive experience of men who have seen the benefit of work-life-balance programs over the years. But the clear majority did not see this as good news.

One of the biggest disconnects between how men and women view things is that, in a man's mind, certain accommodations equate to different people having different standards. And they strongly believe that that equals special treatment. For example, women might not see flextime as a different standard and thus special treatment, but many men do. (On top of that, many men said those accommodations may even add *more* trouble or time to the plate of the nonflextime team members.)

> While women might not see flextime
> as special treatment, many men do.

Many male observers feel that giving special treatment to one person creates its own dilemma: by default, it puts another person at a relative disadvantage. And out of the same desire for fairness that motivates women, the men said anyone should be aware that special treatment is being asked for.

One man compared the situation to a woman playing competitive golf with the guys. She's allowed to hit from the women's tee, which is closer to the green, and sees it as leveling the playing field so she can compete equally. Men see this allowance as unequal. My interviewee mentioned a mutual female friend who is a former Olympian. When she plays golf with men, she plays off the men's tee rather than the women's tee and in doing so earns their astonished respect. But as he pointed out,

> In most cases, women hit off the women's tee and we're
> fine with that. It is an accommodation, but fine. It's sort
> of like that in business—most men aren't at all opposed

to making an accommodation for children or recognizing that a colleague may have a difficult family situation, and cutting her a break. We're not heartless! The problem is, guys don't usually ask for a similar accommodation from other guys. Or if we do, we know it is an accommodation. In golf, a guy who doesn't have as much arm strength as other guys would never ask to hit from the women's tee. And in business, many men would never ask for what some women ask for. We are willing to give her that—it's just that to some men, she's not competing equally. I know this is going to sound harsh, but it's like, if you worked fewer hours and produced less but got the same bonus, I can be pleased for you—but just don't fool yourself into thinking that you got it fair and square.

HOW TO IMPROVE PERCEPTIONS

As a working mom myself, torn every day between the demands of my job and the needs of my two small children, I know that hearing these private male perceptions can be disconcerting or even exasperating. Thankfully, the perceptions I'm passing along are not as negative as they may appear at first glance. Men I interviewed and surveyed said they, too, are torn on this subject, and they recognized that women are often placed in a dilemma since, statistically, women still are more likely to have (or want) primary child-care responsibilities.

That said, no matter how torn men are, they do inherently understand how to manage the way in which they are perceived in this area. And we need to know how to do it too, so we can make the informed decisions that are right for us—especially if our informed decision is to continue to prioritize time and flexibility for our family.

Even though "asking for different standards" can be viewed negatively, men's perceptions can change with several factors. Three things in particular are so powerful that in some cases the different standards become a nonissue.

Acknowledge special treatment is being requested. Men respect when someone accurately assesses the situation and is willing either to acknowledge that they are asking for special treatment and compensate for it in some other way (like serving on the dreaded interdepartment committee in return for working fewer hours on Friday) or to acknowledge that they *may* need to adjust their expectations for projects, pay, and promotions during the period when they can't work as many hours as others.

Adjust expectations along with output. The men emphasized that there is no reason to adjust expectations if someone's production or hours of availability remain unchanged. But if an accommodation goes hand in hand with unequal availability or output, men expect an agreement that differences in compensation, promotion, or opportunity would be understandable if they occur.

However, one often overlooked factor is the opportunities that lead to higher pay and promotion potential. Harold, the Big Four managing partner, provided an illuminating example:

> In a professional services firm like this one, you have three things going on: you have to handle clients, develop people who are coming up, and then you have business development—you have to find new clients. Business development will give you the best pay and advancement, but it's also the most time intensive and unpredictable. Among management, there has been an understanding that there's clearly an uneven playing field between women who historically have to balance family responsibilities and everyone else.
>
> Men would say, "This is a difficult client situation; we

should probably put Joe on it instead of Mary. She has flextime, and if the people underneath have problems and she's not here, I'm going to have to step in." There were sometimes similar issues on personnel development.

The result is that in this office, the ratio of men to women was about fifty-fifty on service delivery, sixty-forty on people development, and by the time you got to business development, it was seventy-five to twenty-five. The women with families could come in and do the work but simply didn't have time to grow the practice.

Adding up those percentages, men would believe that more men than women were qualified, capable, responsible, and deserving at the highest level. And where it starts to rub a little bit is where a guy who works hard and makes partner in twelve years sees a woman take five years off the partnership or business-development track but make partner in thirteen years. There's definitely resentment.

On the other hand, when you look at the broader perspective, you see that if you're going to get women in the workforce, and many of them will have these breaks, it might be fifteen or sixteen years until they make partner—and that just doesn't work. People aren't sitting there with a calendar, saying, "Jane, you lost a busy season here, so you need to pay with an extra year or three." Instead they decide, "Is she ready to move up and can she contribute as a partner?"

The good news is more of these adjusted situations are creating opportunities (such as nonequity partner tracks, or part-time-but-still-integrally-involved roles) for women who actively want to use their skills, but don't want the time pressure and stress of trying to climb the corporate ladder because of family responsibilities.

Realistically account for impact. Of course, when it comes to how men perceive women asking for different standards, everything goes back to the mantra, "It's all about results."

When women accurately estimate the impact of their flexible situation, and ensure that they are able to get the agreed-upon amount of work done on time with no disruption to the team, the perception of a double standard disappears. For example, many men said their perception of flextime improved when they saw workers be willing to adjust their expectations—but then return so much productivity under the flextime arrangement that there was no longer a need to adjust their expectations!

I interviewed one rising-star businesswoman from a Fortune 50 company who had requested, while her kids were young, to work only four days a week, with only three of those days in the office. Nearly everyone else on her team was male, and she said there was a lot of quiet resentment at first. But it vanished when they saw that her numbers remained exactly the same, despite the cut in her work hours. In other words, her productivity had increased, and that protected the team's overall position in the company. It also helped, she said, that she openly acknowledged that her two days of absence from the office made the situation more complicated for those who remained, and she went out of her way to minimize those complications. Because of her approach, her bonus ended up being just as high as that of the other top producers in the office.

So there are good examples. I also heard negative ones. I was surprised at the number of situations where a woman was realistic that she was asking for a special accommodation (such as working from home on Fridays) and willing to adjust her expectations for pay or promotion, but not at all realistic about what would be needed to ensure that her arrangement did not hinder her work or that of the rest of the office. In such cases, the end result was a net negative for everyone. One man mentioned an analyst who regularly overestimated how much work she could get done at home on Fridays during her baby's nap times. She was completely willing to take a cut in pay but was still viewed negatively because she regularly missed deadlines.

As you can see, the common element in each factor that improves how you are perceived is being proactive about the situation. You are demonstrating that you value the team even when your choice is ultimately to prioritize your personal situation. Look at this example from Barry, the COO of a household-name company:

> A few years back, a key female employee came to me and said her eight-year-old daughter was struggling academically at school and was on the verge of being asked to leave. This employee's husband, a busy traveling salesman, simply wasn't home enough to spend extra time with their daughter. So this woman said she needed to switch to a three-and-a-half-day workweek to spend the rest of the workweek at the school, working with her daughter. I moved her down just slightly with regards to her trajectory here, but I thought that it was a sign of great character that she was willing to say, "I know this will affect my career for a few years, but this is more important." I really respected how she handled it.

PUTTING IT IN PERSPECTIVE

In the end, understanding how to navigate the "suck it up" mind-set is only part of the picture. Most working women I know feel that they are already doing more than is humanly possible to meet expectations at work and home. With this in mind, I recommend we give ourselves a break by recognizing several important realities.

There's no perfect solution to balancing work and home

Priorities on the job and with our kids are both important (though not equally so) and often mutually exclusive. They will always compete for our attention, energy, and value. And few answers on what to prioritize and when will work for everyone. Thankfully, we have biblical guidance on how to make the right decision for us. In chapter 9 I discuss a very personal book and Bible study I've put out called *The Life Ready Woman* that helps women do just that.

One thing we know for sure is that wishful thinking about how much we can balance is usually a recipe for anxiety and distress on all fronts. As most working moms (me included) have found, you really can't get that report out on time when you have a five-year old tugging at your sleeve and saying, "Mommy, I'm hungry," or "Mommy, can you play with me now?" And as many of us have also found, being there physically but constantly having to say, "Not right now, honey," leads to heartache for both of you!

> *Wishful thinking about how much we can balance is usually a recipe for anxiety and distress on both fronts.*

We are blessed to live in an era when we can have it all, but as many of us have discovered, it doesn't work to try to have it all, all at the same time. In a 2006 interview with *Time* magazine, a reporter asked Meredith Vieira, "What do you say to women who want to have it all?" Here's her answer:

I hate that expression. When I left *60 Minutes* [to focus on my family], I had women who came up to me very angry and said, "You know, you were proof you could have it all. How dare you leave?" I thought that was ridiculous—

I would lie to myself to create a lie for everybody else? You have to prioritize. If you can fit in job and kids and be comfortable with it, great. At that point, I realized I couldn't do it and give my kids and husband what they needed.[1]

Later, of course, when her children were older, she became a host of *The View* and then the *TODAY Show*. As her example indicates, I believe women will experience less stress when we purposely recognize and plan for the fact that time with one priority may mean not having as much time for the other priority. That way we can actively choose the path that is right for us and our family in a given situation, instead of feeling constantly disappointed by trying to meet our own and others' unrealistic expectations.

Family and career are both enduring desires for women

Women have had this tension ever since we first moved into the professional workplace in great numbers. Harold, the Big Four managing partner, brought this into perspective:

Auditing and consulting are professions that attract a good number of women, and we did these flex work plans thirty years ago. Early on, the firm was 20 to 30 percent female. The last twenty years we've grown to at least 50 percent female. When you realize that more than half your working population is female, you realize you need to do whatever you can to attract and retain them. But all those programs can only help women with the tension of balancing work and family. They don't miraculously solve it.

I have worked with many, many women here who

said, "I'm going to keep working with no change," but when their child was born, they told me that they didn't want to be away that much and needed to leave the firm or have a flex work arrangement. If that is how they felt, I have always taken the position, "You're absolutely right."

I had that conversation in 1975 and two weeks ago. Some things have lasted for thirty-five years, and the internal tension is no different for women today than it was then.

Not every woman experiences the tension, but for those who do it helps to recognize that the desire to spend more time with the kids and the sense that you also have a calling outside the home can both be God given and, as such, are not to be ignored. And as noted earlier, there *is* a way to figure out God's design and callings for you and your family, consistent with the biblical truth that God would never ask us to engage in a work calling that would hurt our family. One key is timing: we are called to steward well all the gifts we've been given, and children in the home are a gift for a limited season. You know the saying: at the end of your life, you are unlikely to lament, "I wish I'd spent more time at the office."

You don't have to give in to the pressure of expectations

Just because certain expectations exist in the workplace doesn't mean we have to meet them, or allow them to pressure us into a course demonstrably not right for us. Some women are comfortable with prioritizing the career fast track and accepting the trade-off to their personal lives. Others are very much not.

And actually, multiple studies over the last ten years show that even highly educated, fast-rising women are becoming less willing to sacrifice time with their families for the sake of career, at least while their children are young. It's likely that at least half of the notorious wage gap between men's and women's wages (where full-time women make eighty cents for every dollar made by men for the same job)[2] can be explained by the fact that many women are in fact choosing (either proactively or by default) the trade-off in wage expectations discussed in this chapter.

One of my close female friends is an example. She's a competent project manager, invaluable to her firm. Now that she has small children, she told her firm she can take on only a limited amount of travel. By contrast, her male peer at the firm took his job knowing it would require quite a large amount of travel, including long international trips away from his own family. Not surprisingly, my friend realistically knows her peer will be paid more for that extra work sacrifice, and she is fine with that. The discrepancy between their wages is counted as part of the wage gap of unequal pay for equal work, when, in fact, it reflects different pay for different work.[3]

THERE IS GOOD NEWS

Although some old problems stubbornly persist, some previously entrenched workplace expectations appear to be slowly changing. The men I interviewed frequently said old-guard expectations are not best for them either. Many expressed regret about being beholden to face-time expectations in the office; expectations they described as not only unhealthy but sometimes unnecessary and unproductive too.

> *Men frequently said old-guard expectations are not best for them either.*

For example, one highly successful male entrepreneur who runs a private venture-capital fund described his own choice:

My daughters are all teens and preteens now, and I realized that these are the last years they will be living at home. Other people can do things at the office if necessary, but nobody else can be a dad to my girls. So I throttled back the pursuit of my business ambition over the next five years, so I can get things right at home. I haven't said, "I'm going to try to have everything that I want in my business *and* at home." Sure, I'd love to make the same income I did last year, but you can't have it all. So I have made a conscious decision to trade off. There is no doubt that workaholics and totally driven people usually do better in business, but those people have a trade-off at home, sometimes a serious one. I don't want to run my life like that.

It would be ironic if we traded away our hard-won ability to make choices just to fit old-guard beliefs that desperately need to be changed to begin with. And most of the time, we don't need to. While the tension between family and career will likely always be with us, and there will always be some who feel pressured to (as the venture capitalist put it) "have a trade-off at home," recent studies have documented increasing numbers of both women and men who are championing an alternative workplace model—and an alternative workplace perception. Not through the sort of wishful thinking that is ultimately damaging to self, family, and career, but through the clear-eyed decision to prioritize what is most important and then doing what we choose to do, well.

CHAPTER 6

"I'm Not as Confident as I Look"

Men's Inner Insecurity and Need for Respect

Remember my in-flight conversation at the opening of the book with a leadership consultant who, a few hours before, had watched a female executive unintentionally make a poor impression with her male colleagues?

The story he told me described a seemingly trivial situation, but it points to something larger that women easily miss. He had been at an all-day meeting at a well-known sports-related corporation, where thirty of the company's senior executives took turns presenting business strategies for the next year. Most of the executives were men, with a sprinkling of women. The strategy session took place on the same day that major sports-related news was breaking, and from time to time someone would crack open the door and gesture to an executive in the room that they were needed outside for a moment.

Apparently, this happened several times while a female senior vice president, whom I'll call Carol, was making her presentation. Several times Carol glanced sideways, gave a small sigh of exasperation at being interrupted, then continued.

At the end of the day, after the others had left, the consultant was working with the CEO and the COO. An executive vice president slot was about to open up, and ideally they wanted to fill it with one of the people who had been in the room that day. They looked at the profile of each senior vice president in detail, and none were really feasible, until they came to Carol. This consultant was thrilled to see she had exactly the experience and skill set needed. Plus the corporation had been actively trying to move more women into leadership.

"Carol is perfect," he told the CEO. "She's got the right education, capabilities, and you'd get all these connections with partner companies—"

The CEO regretfully shook his head. "We can't promote her. I wish we could."

"Why not?"

"Well...did you see what happened when she was interrupted? That little sigh of annoyance? She has a tendency to make every man she works with feel like an idiot. She would be a negative presence on the executive team."

The consultant told me he didn't understand why Carol would shoot herself in the foot like that. But in talking with me about the male-female disconnect, he realized she probably didn't recognize what she was doing.

So what was she doing? What made every man she worked with feel like an idiot? Why would something so subtle as a small sigh of exasperation be described as representative of a "negative presence," a description with which the male consultant immediately agreed?

The answer to those questions can best be understood in light of a single finding of my research: 76 percent of the men I interviewed agreed that they sometimes or regularly feel "I'm not always as confident as I look."[1]

Behind this simple, seemingly innocuous finding is a complex truth about men, one that requires venturing deep into the emotional landscape of the male psyche. One that will give you a completely different perspective on the men in your office and open your eyes to small changes that will have a big impact on creating positive, rewarding, and God-honoring workplace relationships. Let's take a look.

TOUCHING A HIDDEN INSECURITY NERVE

Women observe how men interact with the world and conclude that some men have an inflated view of themselves. We blame that on what we call the male ego. Yet underneath the external confidence that men project is a more complicated reality.

Aidan, a male partner in a global consulting firm who manages a large number of women, provides a vital clue:

> Men and women equally want to get ahead. But in the corporate world, a man's ego is a much bigger issue.... You can give women feedback and they'll take it well. Women can help people work as a team and not see everyone as a threat. But women also tend to forget that not everyone is like them. The one universal thing is a man's ego—and the heart of that is fear.

In my survey, most men echoed what I regularly heard in interviews: they often felt like an impostor. In fact, seven out of ten men on the survey said no matter how much confidence they projected, they sometimes or regularly felt lost. They think, *I hope I can figure this thing out before someone realizes I'm not sure what I'm doing!*[2] That sense of uncertainty veers uncomfortably close to feeling inadequate—an unusually painful feeling for a man and one that he prefers to avoid at all costs.

I believe understanding this inner uncertainty explains many frustrating dynamics that women encounter in the workplace. For example, the double standard that strong men are "assertive" while strong women are "difficult" (or worse). Men instinctively understand that they all suffer from self-doubt at times, no matter how much confidence they project. So they have built a type of unspoken social contract, where they instinctively avoid hitting that nerve in other men. If they do hit it, they are often doing so on purpose, to deliberately undermine the other guy, knowing exactly what they've done and why.

Unfortunately, few women seem to recognize this hidden self-doubt and the underlying social contract that goes with it. As a result, we are far more likely to say things in a way that another man never would, create hard feelings or a poor perception, and even become someone that men go out of their way to avoid—without ever realizing it.

If we do sense hard feelings, we tend to dismiss them, attributing them to the man in question being oversensitive or feeling threatened by the presence of a strong, capable woman. It may be helpful for women to realize that most men are "oversensitive" in this way, but not just with us. They are oversensitive with one another, as well, which is why they've built up these expectations of how colleagues should interact and relate.

WHEN HIS DEEP FEAR MEETS
HIS INTENSE NEED

Men's underlying self-doubt and sensitivity in the workplace suggests a host of complex implications for women. But my research identified two powerful interlocking feelings or needs behind this vulnerability, of which women need to be especially aware.

Feeling 1: Even though men seek challenges, they live with a deep fear they'll be seen as inadequate to meet them

Most men thrive on tackling new challenges, regardless of how many bumps and bruises come their way. The same instinct that compels my kindergarten-age son to hurtle himself down ten stairs and try to land on his feet compels adult men to tackle a workplace version of the same challenge.

In Work World, however, the stakes are no longer physical, but emotional. What is at stake is not, "Will I break an ankle?" but, "Will someone discover that I am not adequate to the task?" That leads to an inherent male tension, because for a man the feeling of, or fear of, inadequacy is not just uncomfortable, it is his most painful sensation.

Remember the earlier comment by Aidan, the change management partner? "The one universal thing is a man's ego—and the heart of that is fear."

Thanks to testosterone and an aggression-oriented brain structure, men have a biological bent toward wanting to push things forward in the face of daunting obstacles. Author John Eldredge memorably described this as a man's God-given, "wild at heart" nature. As one man put it, "Men judge success by doing something, period. If you're able to do it, you're successful, and your degree of success is also easily measured." But this is complicated by the very unique male need to do and figure those things out alone. As a Christian businessman and manager named Sean told me, "No guy wants to admit he does not have an answer. That is why guys try and solve everything on their own. Asking for help is a sign of weakness and failure. They don't ever want to admit they are not up to the task, and they think they can make themselves up to the task, so they sometimes take on tasks they are not capable of doing easily."

Not surprisingly, a man who lives with the tension of wanting to leap forward but wanting to avoid failure in the eyes of others finds that fear of possible humiliation always on his shoulder. One C-level executive explained, "A man's greatest fear is being seen as incompetent."

Sean had spent years rising through the ranks at a huge company. He'd also made a ministry of mentoring dozens of other successful businessmen. Yet when we sat in his New York office behind a closed door, he gave me example after example of how isolated these men often felt. He said, "As they get up the ladder, they have fears and private failures and this fear of being exposed, but no one to share with. The insecurity is that you'll be found out as incompetent. That at some point someone is going to turn over a leaf and realize, 'This guy has no idea what he is doing.'"

> *"The insecurity is that you'll be found incompetent, that at some point someone is going to realize, 'This guy has no idea what he is doing.'"*

Here's a perspective from a fast-rising broadcasting executive:

When I was younger I used to feel invincible: I can do anything! Now, I sit in this office and I go, *I cannot believe that I am here.* I feel like somebody is going to walk in and say, "What are you doing here? Get out of here, you don't belong here!" That sense of invincibility has disappeared over time, because the higher up you get, the more you see all of the different pitfalls and all the things that you do not know—and that you have to rely on other people for. In fact, now I rely almost entirely on everybody else, which then makes you think that you are even more of a fraud, because you are not an expert in any of the substantive areas anymore! I recently heard a retired CEO confess to a similar feeling during his years at the top, and that was actually a relief to hear.

On all my surveys, regardless of how I asked the question, roughly three-quarters of men admitted to self-doubt or fear. On the main workplace survey, in one question regarding what types of insecurity they experienced, if any, 74 percent said one or more applied to them, particularly concerns about how they were viewed by others or their employability in their workplace.[3] It is worth noting that this survey was conducted in 2008, when the market was at a high point and jobs were plentiful, *before* the economy and employment fell off a cliff.

Feeling 2: Even though men fear their own inadequacy, they live with an intense emotional need to feel respected

We all want to be respected in the workplace. But for most men, this is not just a want, but an intense, even desperate, emotional need.

In my book *For Women Only*, three out of four men on the survey about their personal relationships said that if they had to make a choice, they would give up feeling loved, to feel respected and adequate. "I'll feel unloved if I have to," one man said. "Just don't make me feel inadequate."

How this translates to the workplace is that men want and are more motivated by respect, trust, and appreciation than by, for example, whether someone likes them or enjoys working with them. This explains why sometimes men brush off things women might take personally, yet get defensive about other issues that wouldn't bother us.

Despite men's claim that one shouldn't take things personally in business, this is one of the things they seem much more likely to take personally than women, even if they never show it. As one Christian businessman told me,

> Most men couldn't care less whether someone likes or dislikes them unless it serves a business purpose. But they care deeply whether someone respects them. I know that I keep many of my customers simply because they like me and enjoy working with me, but it really doesn't matter if my co-worker in the next cube seems to dislike me. I'd prefer cordial relationships, but it matters more that he knows I'm the guy who will get the job done.

And sensing that respect makes a big impression. As one man explained, "My assessment of an individual is not impacted by whether or not this person likes me or will like me, but it is heavily impacted by whether I think this person does or doesn't respect me."

It is worth noting that several men brought up a downside to this dynamic. Ronald, the prominent COO quoted in an earlier chapter, said, "Being liked is often a business good that we miss; it is why women sometimes work harder to seek the win-wins than the men do. A man is sometimes too focused on his own performance and competing for the win, and whether the other party thinks he is good at his job."

One of the main reasons men crave respect is because it mitigates their underlying sense of insecurity. One day, out with several other couples for dinner, two friends who are well-regarded businessmen ended up talking about this relationship between respect and insecurity. One man, whom I will call Gary, offered a vivid metaphor:

Insecurity is sort of like having a bad back, where the disability is chronic. You've learned to live with it. You don't like it, but you do things to compensate. Disrespect is where someone comes along and slugs you right on the sensitive part of your back and the pain is sharp. You can manage the constant ache of the insecurity, but you're going to do whatever you can to avoid that intense pain.

SEVEN SIGNALS MEN SEE AS DISRESPECT

This gets to the heart of the issue: Men are aware that they share a finely tuned disrespect radar and know how to avoid triggering it. But if a woman is not conscious of men's sensitivity, she can send damaging signals without realizing it.

Even what women might view as a minor comment could loom

large in a man's mind, if he assumes it's a signal of how she views him overall. Similarly, women might view a particular comment or concern as isolated, thinking, *I respect my boss in all these areas, but just not in that one.* For many men, though, it doesn't work that way. In their minds, the other person either respects them and their overall judgment (even if he or she disagrees with them on certain points), or only respects them when they do something perfectly, which means he or she doesn't really respect them at all.

As one business owner wryly confirmed, "Yes, men can see disrespect where none is intended. This is a skill that we have. An ability we have evolved."

That sensitivity, combined with what many men described as having their identity wrapped up with their work—where respect is expected as the default rule—means men at work are likely to have a particularly negative, though hidden, knee-jerk reaction to perceived disrespect or inadequacy. The most common reaction: unexpressed irritation or anger—anger kept under wraps because showing such emotions would violate one of the other common expectations of the workplace, which is that you remain levelheaded and don't take things personally. Sometimes, in fact, a man isn't even sure why he's irritated. One man told me,

> Until you and I talked about this feeling of inadequacy,
> I didn't know where to put this feeling I tend to have
> around this one female associate, but this issue is exactly
> it. When she says in that sort of comforting, overly patient
> tone, "Doug, don't worry, we'll get there," it seems like she
> is talking down to me. I would not have been able to put a
> finger on it, and I certainly would never have been able to
> explain it to her.

Many men said even when they do identify what they feel as inadequacy or disrespect, they push it down because they "shouldn't feel that way." Yet they remain wary of the source of that painful feeling, and that wariness makes them likely to see signals of disrespect in the future.

So what exactly do men perceive as disrespect in the first place? Many disrespectful signals are obvious. The key, for us, is to understand the most common *unintentional* ones. And as dozens of men told me, "It is not what you say, but how you say it" that matters. (Especially since, many admitted, some men are simply more sensitive to signs of disrespect from women than from another man.)

Here is how Aidan put it: "Everyone needs to be able to ask questions or challenge potential problems. It is not *that* you question me, but *how* you question me that makes me think you are questioning my ability to lead this practice area. For example, if it is done to try to understand, then that is a whole lot easier than stating your point of view assertively."

Here are seven "how you do it" situations that men (and some women, for that matter), are likely to perceive as signs that you view them as inadequate.

Signal 1: A direct, brusque approach

Surprisingly (and contrary to much of the advice women receive during business coaching), it is easy for men to experience a direct approach, especially a question, as a confrontation or an attack. I got a great example of this when I had the first working session with my survey designer, Chuck Cowan, on the personal-relationship survey questions in *For Women Only*. I had drafted a question for the men that read, "Do you know how to put together a romantic event that your wife would enjoy?"

I was completely mystified when Chuck said, "That question won't work because you're starting off in attack mode."

Huh? I thought.

"You're starting off suggesting the man is inept," he insisted.

I thought, *Suggesting the man is inept? What is he talking about?*

Chuck's suggestion: "Soften it a bit. Put it in a context that isn't so blatant."

Simply by adding a context sentence to the beginning ("Suppose you had to plan a romantic event for your wife. Do you know how...?"), the very same question was no longer perceived as an attack on a man's adequacy.

When I politely challenged the notion that women are more brusque (since I'd seen plenty of male directness along the way!), every man I interviewed said essentially the same thing: men are direct, yes, but most men purposefully do not *confront*, unless they are trying to throw the other person off balance. So we need to know what they can see as simply "direct" versus "confrontational." One executive made this distinction:

> First, a man will be far more direct one on one than he would be in front of others. In a group, such directness would be public humiliation. But even when it is one on one, a male manager will be direct in a way a guy can hear. He'll say, "Bob, you've hit us some great home runs this past year, and I'm still in awe of how you landed the Hansel deal—but this was one boneheaded move on the Greene merger. How are you going to fix it?" In a group, though, he will find a way to be direct but not make it a confrontation. He'll say something like, "I'm still in awe of how you landed the Hansel deal, but you missed this one on the Greene merger. So let's figure out how to scramble to fix it." He'll convey his message that way unless he's the sort of guy who rules by fear and is trying for a scorched-earth approach. Or unless he has no social skills.

Signal 2: Believing a decision wasn't based on a legitimate reason

I daresay that each of us, whether at work or in personal life, has at some point said in frustration, "What was he (or she) thinking?" The translation of that, of course, is, "He wasn't thinking." When that assumption creeps into our conscious or subconscious thoughts in the workplace, it can quickly lead to words or actions that anyone, man or woman, legitimately perceives as disrespectful, because our underlying assumption is indeed a disrespectful one. Take a look at this representative example:

UNINTENDED DISRESPECT AS SEEN BY A SENIOR PARTNER OF A $1 BILLION CONSULTING FIRM

In our area, we have a few partners like me, in their forties or fifties, and a lot of eager, up-and-coming associates. One junior associate, Wendy, has a lot of potential, but she caused a huge headache last summer when I chose not to bring her on a sales situation. In our business, the partner going to a client-development meeting picks one associate to go along. Those opportunities are rare, and every associate wants to be the one invited, because helping land deals is how you get ahead.

We had taken on a contractor in his fifties, Drew, for a few months' work. Near the end of his three-month contract, I landed a big sales meeting and took him with me. Wendy was offended that she didn't get to go—but she told others, not me. I heard afterward that she had been talking to a few colleagues about not getting to go and she resented that she'd been busting her tail for two years and hadn't been to many sales meetings, and he's not even an employee, but he's older and a man, and he gets to go.

Obviously, I thought she was questioning my judgment. She thought I was biased and had favorites, that I didn't have a legitimate reason for what I did. The fact that she didn't even come to me and *ask* implies that she doesn't think she'd get a fair hearing. Very disrespectful. Not to mention that she told others. If I needed to question a man's decision, I would do it one to one and make sure he knew I had his best interest at heart. I would only question him to others if I wanted to undermine him.

It would have completely changed my perception of Wendy if she had come to me and said, "I'm sure you've made the right decision here, but I just want to understand why." I would have told her, in confidence, that I was trying to decide whether to take on Drew full-time. In his three months, I had seen him in every other situation, and this would be my only chance to see how he did in a sales situation. And based on his performance that day, I decided not to hire him.

Even if Wendy wasn't comfortable coming in straight on and saying, "Help me understand this," she still could have addressed it while avoiding the specific example. She could have said, "I'd like to go with you to a sales situation; this is important to me, so I'm going to keep asking about this." I would think, *She probably saw me taking Drew. And I respect the fact that she's not taking me to task for that. That she respects my decision and trusts me with it, even if she didn't know what my reasoning was.*

Even when you are risk averse and don't want to confront the other person directly, you need to state what you want: "I'd love to go to more selling situations. I know you're a great salesperson and so the next sales situation you get, I'd like to go with you." That flattery works incredibly well with guys. And if the guy is at all smart, he'll understand what she's not saying.

Quite a few men expressed frustration at any assumption by women who worked for them that their hiring, pay, promotion, or project-allocation decisions were affected by anti-female bias instead of legitimate business reasons. While gender discrimination is indeed still a real issue in some workplaces, it was surprising that a number of men who were clearly women's advocates could recount examples of women who saw even them as biased. That signal of distrust, they said, not surprisingly, caused them to view those women negatively.

Malcolm, the president of a well-known midsize company, gave this example:

> I've been in lots of different roles over twenty years and I've honestly never seen [hiring or promoting discrimination] here, yet our female HR director is convinced it happens all the time. I can tell her we've spent all this time and money to add more women in leadership, and this just bounces off her.
>
> Recently, we were looking at candidates for a key person to network with our grassroots customer groups. Our four final candidates were two white women, a white man, and a black man. The senior VP and leadership group making the decision are in their thirties and forties, and are totally gender blind. They are looking for competency, period. Of the four candidates, the black man was offered the job because he already had tons of these relationships and would hit the ground running.
>
> So our HR director says, "It's a gender issue." Whenever we have made a hiring decision away from a female candidate, our HR director claims it's not simply about competency but because "you guys play golf together." The irony is we've got fourteen people on the executive team,

and I think only four of them play golf, but that was one of the rumors that got started: "You have to play golf here to get ahead."

As you might imagine, Malcolm and the executive team preferred not to work with an HR director whom they perceived as constantly distrustful of their decisions. A year after my interview, she left the organization, never recognizing that her open distrust of leadership had caused any problems for her.

Signal 3: Asking, "Why?"

This is one of the most common ways women unintentionally signal they distrust a colleague's judgment. When we ask something like, "Bob, why did you choose that pricing?" or "Why is this our strategy here?" we are usually simply seeking information. Yet all too often, especially if it is asked in front of others, men hear even the most benignly phrased "Why?" as a challenge.

Men surveyed said if they were making a proposal in a group situation and a colleague began asking why, they would likely assume that colleague was trying to understand. However, nearly two in three said they might *also* feel that "my colleague is questioning my judgment." (Forty-two percent said it would depend on who was asking.)

In one focus group, a man I'll call Neil provided an example that hit home with the businesswomen who were also in the group that day. Neil is an executive who specializes in growing businesses. He is also even keeled and tends to get along with everyone, making his story even more of a surprise:

When I was commuting to Seattle to run a consumer products business, there was a woman I worked with

who...well...I just didn't like her. It really became an issue
with me, and I couldn't put my finger on why. I'd even be
on the phone with my wife and she'd ask, "Are you okay?"
I'd say, "I'm fine." She'd pause, then ask, "Were you in a
meeting with Nicole?"

Finally my wife tried to help me reconstruct things:
"Why don't you like Nicole?"

I realized eventually what it was. I don't think Nicole
disrespected me, but I read disrespect because in our
meetings she would always ask "why" questions. Instead
of asking "what" or "how," it was very much, "But why do
you think that?" I felt that she was questioning me, and
it was very offensive to me.

And finally when I told this to my wife, she said,
"She's not challenging you; she's trying to understand. It
helps her understand." I'm like, "Really?" It took awhile
before that sank in, and eventually Nicole and I ended
up becoming fast friends. A year later, over dinner, I said,
"You know, Nicole, you really ticked me off when we first
started working together."

She said, "I know,...but why?"

"Because I always felt you were challenging my
position."

"But you know I wouldn't do that!"

I had to laugh. "No, I didn't know. That was the
whole point!"

Interestingly, my feeling disrespected by her never
occurred in a one-on-one situation. It was only when I
felt she was challenging me in front of others in a larger
meeting. One on one, if she asked, "Why?" it wouldn't
bother me. But in a meeting, it created a very different
dynamic.

In the focus group where Neil told his story, the businesswomen in the room raised the natural follow-up concern: "If asking 'Why?' can be heard incorrectly, how should the question be asked?" Also, "Is it that women are more likely to ask, 'Why?' or that men are more bothered by it when a woman asks?"

One man in the focus group answered by saying that the actual word *why* is used by women far more than by men.

Another man said, "Guys will ask the same question, but we will do it in a different way so that we avoid the word 'why.' We'll say, 'I'm not following the reason for setting it up that way.'"

A third man added, "Or, 'Can you tell me what you're thinking here?'"

The second man said it clearly mattered more when the question was raised in front of others and suggested saying instead, "Help me understand where you're going on this one." He added, "It's the equivalent of saying, 'I know you are going somewhere with this and do have a reason. Help me understand what it is.'"

But the first man experienced it in one-on-one meetings, as well. He said, "For example, yesterday, after I got a verbal agreement from a customer, my VP came into my office and asked, 'Why did you agree to this price?' To me, she's not just asking a question; she's saying I didn't do my job. She's questioning my judgment as a salesperson. It would have been totally different if she would have said, 'I've got to understand your thinking on this.'"

"Or," another man chimed in, "'Help me understand your reasoning on this deal,' not—"

All the men laughed and said in unison, "'WHY?!'"

Signal 4: Pushing too much

Quite a number of men raised pushing as an issue: when someone disagrees with their decision, and won't let it go or too forcefully presses to change it, they hear a challenge to their authority or judgment. Disagreement itself doesn't convey disrespect, they said. The key is the other person's manner and length of time in expressing it. In their experience, women were more likely to "push" than a man. Ironically, many women I interviewed agreed.

> *Disagreement itself doesn't convey disrespect. The key is the other person's manner and length of time in expressing it.*

Kevin, the human resources director quoted in earlier chapters, gave this example:

> Several women who worked for me over the years would argue opinions until I could not take it anymore. I am not the type that is just going to say, "We are going to do it my way." If I feel strongly about something, I am going to let you see my rationale and all the reasons why I think this is right. Usually, people come around to, "Okay, I disagree, but I get your perspective and understand why you want to do it this way." But several of these women wouldn't. They finally had to tell me, "You just need to tell me to do it your way because you are the boss." Which is totally not my style. My first thought in these situations is, *Why can't this person wrap her mind around this topic and see it in another way? Why is she dead set on being right?* Then what goes through my brain is, *She does not respect my opinion.*

Signal 5: Exasperation

Clear exasperation would make anyone feel disrespected. It's also unprofessional and, I would have thought, rare. So I was surprised at the number of times men brought it up. I eventually realized that what men were talking about were nonverbal, body-language cues, presumably unintentional, and mostly given by women.

One C-level executive at a well-known multinational printing company said, "Men are not affected by body language by other men, but they are very attuned to the body language of women."

A university administrator explained,

> Exasperation is something you feel for your toddler when he throws his third tantrum in the store. No man wants to feel that he's being treated like a three-year-old. Even the most subtle roll of the eyes will do it, whether it is his wife or his female colleague. You will almost never see a man in a work setting make an exasperated sound, roll his eyes, or listen with crossed arms and an irritated look on his face. You do see a few women. It never works out well for them.

This is also the answer to why, in our opening story, the female executive's small sound of exasperation at being interrupted was viewed so poorly. It was apparently just part of a pattern of behavior that made, in the words of the CEO, "every man she worked with feel like an idiot." And it cost her the promotion to EVP.

Signal 6: Micromanagement

Overmanaging can make anyone feel disrespected, but it is worth mentioning here because quite a few men raised it as an issue with women—and provided examples I would not have seen as micromanagement. One man said,

> Micromanagement can sometimes be subtle. If she wants to be included in everything, or is offended at being left out, that's a lack of trust. It is partially why women more often write a long e-mail versus a guy who writes one line.

It's not that we, as guys, are incapable of thinking through the same paragraphs and providing clarification. It's that we trust the person receiving the e-mail. Most of the time, guys are going to feel like they can understand why they are getting this e-mail without the extra three paragraphs.

Signal 7: Direct disagreement

Direct disagreement—and sometimes even making suggestions in a group setting—can be easily misperceived. The key is the manner of expressing it. When I asked Toby, a partner in a midsize, Christian-run advertising company, whether he had seen female colleagues do things misperceived by men, he said, "Any type of corrective actions or corrective suggestions, like, 'You need to go more in this direction,' or 'You need to think about this a different way,' or 'You need to focus on the important, not the urgent.'" Toby said it makes a guy think, *Are you threatening my job?* I was surprised that corrective suggestions could be perceived that way. Toby explained,

> It is entirely about how the corrective suggestions are given. "You need to" is rarely a good start. That is more difficult for a man to take from a woman because he immediately tends to relate that to his personal situation, and it drives a guy nuts when his wife says that. It is totally unfair to his female colleague that his mind goes there, but it is better if she realizes that it might. She could just as easily have said, "I know these things are urgent, but we can't afford to miss these more important ones. Let's tackle these first."

Open disagreements are even more charged. I asked Hugh, the sales director for a $1 billion manufacturing company, what he would suggest for a woman who had an actual criticism or disagreement with her male boss. Here's how he answered:

Bottom line, the man needs to feel she is saying, "I respect your ideas. I just don't necessarily agree with them in this case." Some guys will still take the straightforward approach: "That idea stinks, but what about this?" Men can be sensitive to that approach from other men but won't say it. But they can be especially sensitive to that approach from women. So if the woman walks in and doesn't like something, it would benefit her to develop the skill set to say that in a way men can hear.

> *"Bottom line, the man needs to feel that she is saying, 'I respect your ideas. I just don't necessarily agree with them in this case.'"*

One business owner interrupted our interview to take a call from his lead software developer, and when he put down the phone said, "That was a perfect example of how men tend to approach other men. I had told my developer I wanted to do something one way, and he just said, 'Can I offer a suggestion for how we might do it differently?'"

Hugh provided this advice for anyone—but especially any woman working with a male boss:

> Know where you want to go and ask the right question at the right time to lead him down the path to get there. To help him realize that this is where he needs to go. Whether the decision maker is a man or a woman, the best ideas are the ones the boss can develop and get invested in. If you can deliver up your solution in a way that is more palatable, he can seize on it.
>
> I recently proposed a new sales organizational structure, and one of my women sales leaders didn't like it. She

thought I didn't have enough sales leaders to manage the sales reps. But she didn't tell me that right away, and she didn't say, "You're wrong." Instead, she said, "You know, I was looking at your suggestions and seeing you wanted a ratio of one sales leader to eight sellers. What's your reasoning on that?" So it's obvious she's not quite on the same page, without saying so. After I told her my reasons, she asked, "Have you done a work/time study to find out how much time a sales leader spends in the field? That might help us find out whether the sales leader actually has time to manage eight people. I can do that if you'd like."

I said, "Great suggestion. Go and do it." So she came up with the facts to show that we needed a different ratio, and that is what I mean by helping the man adapt to it for himself. Be more of a partner, instead of challenging him head on. Do it in a nonthreatening way, because as soon as he feels that challenge, he shuts down. The window shade is down. And then it becomes a battle of the wills, and he's got the title, so shut up and do it. But asking the question and then listening works really well. It's what I train all my salespeople to do to close a sale, after all. If a woman develops that skill set, she will do very well, especially since women tend to be able to listen better anyway.

THE ART (AND ADVANTAGES) OF GIVING RESPECT

As you can tell from many of these stories, men have an obvious appreciation for those who make a point of showing their respect, especially when concerns or criticisms are raised. Just as men can be overly sensitive to feeling inadequate, they can be deeply attuned to signs of respect.

Here is what they see as three of the most important signals of respect.

A colleague's appreciation is not impacted by occasional mistakes

One key for many men is feeling that the other person's respect is not conditional, but rather a lasting appreciation for their overall competency that won't change in the face of an occasional mistake.

Remember the female associate who undermined her perception with her managing partner when she assumed he was biased for taking an older male contractor on a sales call instead of her? Later in the same interview, the partner went on to share an example of a very different reaction from a woman when *he* was the one who made a mistake.

ONE INCIDENT OF BEING "BRAVE...IN A RESPECTFUL WAY"

We were at a big meeting with multiple offices of our firm and talking about our business lines for the following year. We had five business lines all presenting and competing for resources, and I was feeling pretty competitive since I know I'm a good presenter and I had a fantastic team of people behind me—most of whom were women. But I had poor judgment that day. I had a list of our distinctives, and then I jokingly added, "And my team is much better looking than any other team."

After the meeting, someone on my team had the guts to walk into my office and say, "You have always told us you want feedback. I appreciate how you have fought for women at this firm, but what you just did today perpetuated the sense that women are there to be looked at."

She was totally right, and I had to go apologize to each of the women on my team. And I thought, *If she had the guts to tell me something I didn't want to hear, that makes me think that she is brave and that anything she says is likely to be good and honest.* She didn't try to undermine me in front of others, she didn't lodge a complaint with the other partners, and she didn't imply that I was inherently biased. She respected my advocacy of women enough to point out a way that I had undermined it and then trusted me to make it right. Which, hopefully, I tried to do.

That fast-tracked the relationship with me—that one incident of being brave and giving me some genuine feedback, but in a respectful way.

As an investor-relations executive put it, "What the man wants is to *be* respected, not treated with respect as if an actor has learned his lines. He does best when you expect the best of him."

> "That fast-tracked her relationship with me—that one incident of being brave and giving me some genuine feedback, but in a respectful way."

Clearly, not everyone has that sort of fundamental respect for their co-workers or bosses. I asked the executive how a woman might navigate such a situation. He chuckled and said,

There are limits to transparency. The worst thing she can do for her career if she doesn't respect a male colleague or superior is to make that clear. I'm guessing even in that situation, she can find things to respect. Maybe he's the classic visionary head honcho who is all over the place, has no operational ability, and is constantly messing up the operations people. She can still admire the fact that he's a man of vision and has entrepreneurial drive. She can still respect the person. If you can't find anything to respect, well, respect his position. He's still the boss.

A colleague respects and affirms him in front of others

One thing I frequently heard mentioned is a man's appreciation for someone who shows genuine appreciation in front of others. A senior businessman in the public-relations field, Ferdinand, explained why he deeply respects a female colleague with whom he works closely:

> Claudia is totally willing to acknowledge that my strengths complement certain weaknesses she has. She is slightly senior to me in her role here, but I've had longer tenure in the industry. So there could be tension between us, but there isn't, largely because she is so careful to make me feel my greater experience is appreciated. In public meetings with clients, she will acknowledge that "Ferdinand is the one who is detail oriented, so he will take care of this operational piece." That is also important in our staff meetings, because my personality is low key and Claudia tends to jump over me sometimes, so the junior staff could always perceive her as the only leader.

A male communications specialist who had recently switched firms provided another example. "In my last job, my boss was a woman, and she was totally safe. I could talk to her, share ways I'd messed up, get her input for going forward. It was a very productive situation." When I asked him what his previous boss did that made him feel "safe," he said, "I felt like she was for me. She would brag on my behalf to her peers in the firm. Or tell potential clients about things I had done." In his current firm, he said, he worked almost entirely with women—but he didn't get any of those affirmation signals to let him know whether or not they thought he was doing a good job. As a result, he told me, "I can't share with anyone what I am thinking. I am afraid for them to know."

A colleague's objections are voiced respectfully, not as a challenge

Most of the men I interviewed had enormous respect for women who were able to stand strong on a particular issue, raise objections, or completely disagree in an inoffensive way. Men are grateful to have a professional business interaction that does not contain a subtle undercurrent of questioning their adequacy, but instead allows them to single-mindedly tackle a situation purely on its merits.

Several times, they shared how certain female colleagues seemed to have a "chip on the shoulder," which privately made me wonder if these men were prejudiced against women. Shortly thereafter, however, each man gave examples that proved otherwise. One such man in a large ministry provided this helpful story about a woman who handled well a vital meeting with a group of men far senior to her, by being strong but respectful, and focusing on the business at hand:

> We'd just gone through the budgeting process, and our
> CIO could not attend this critical one-day session, so he
> sent his right-hand person, Teresa, who is thirty-some-
> thing. She's in this annual executive budget meeting with

ten senior executives who are all men, going through a very tough discussion of how we will allocate $240 million, and the big issue is IT, which she represents. I was totally impressed at the way she stood toe to toe with these guys, to the point that I thought to myself, *She is someone to watch.* I saw really good leadership. She didn't kowtow, she didn't back out, and she didn't get harsh. She was calm and bold, gutsy, and would say, "Well, I have to disagree with you on that one, because of X, Y, and Z." Everyone said later, "I really respect the way she handled that." The common thread: "Man, she was *good.*"

I said, "That's what a guy would say about another guy!"
"Exactly!"

THE BENEFIT OF A DIFFERENT APPROACH

Most corporate training and business coaching for women does a good job bolstering confidence and effectiveness in the workplace. But it can subtly backfire, if it doesn't take into account how a given approach will be perceived by male colleagues who are dealing with their own doubts and insecurities.

I stumbled across an example of this several years ago, after I'd already done hundreds of interviews with men. I was looking at a website with popular business coaching tools, including online videos for women in business. Clicking on one at random, I watched a well-known female coach say, "Women, you've got to be aggressive, you've got to be assertive! No one in business is going to give you anything. If you want that corner office, you have to take it!"

Staring at the screen, I could practically hear the echo of hundreds of male voices in my head saying, "Yes, but…!"

In a coffee shop a week later, I showed that video to a male executive whom I have known for years, someone who is an advocate of women in the workplace. His reaction?

> I think women in business need to do all those things the
> corporate trainers suggest. They shouldn't assume anyone
> is going to hand them anything. They should be aware;
> they should be assertive. The question is *how*. Business
> still is, unfortunately, very male-centric. But if women
> understand how men are wired, they can be the type of
> star that others will want to bring through the ranks with
> them.

Several men I interviewed raised another intriguing point, that just as men have natural inclinations and perceptions, so do women. And some of those inclinations (such as the often-mentioned "natural listening ability" or "desire to be liked") could be a benefit in trying to navigate the minefield of male sensitivity in the workplace—and in gaining men's trust.

One COO of a very well-known organization gave this example:

> The desire and need to be liked seems to be greater in
> women. Not all women, of course. But many women in
> business have been made to feel that is a bad thing, totally
> inappropriate in business. I think it is totally rational.
> Women instinctively realize that if they aren't liked, the
> cards are really stacked against them in a male-centered
> environment. So they figure how to confront problems,
> yet still be appreciated. In an environment with male
> egos, a woman who does that will find it a much greater
> value than being a tough contrarian. As long as she is not
> prioritizing being liked over the good of the business, if

it is her genuine personality, she doesn't have to try to squash it. Because that is a strength she can use to offset what is, at times, a man's weakness.

Geoff, the CMO, advised, "Learn how men communicate. Once a man extends real opportunity, figure out how to be influential without being threatening. It's a delicate art, not a science." He said it's understanding what words to pick, what body language to use, what tone to use in your writing. "But," he added, "women are particularly well-suited to do that. And once you figure it out, you're in."

CHAPTER 7

"That Low-Cut Blouse Undercuts Her Career"

Sending the Right Signals and Avoiding the Visual Trap

As I'm writing these words, I'm sitting at a café in a bustling business area, watching an interesting dynamic unfold at a table nearby. Around me in the lunch rush, several groups are continuing business discussions over their soups and salads. At the table across from me, a stylish, thirty-something woman is eating with three men, arguing a passionate point that has something to do with risk management.

But I'm betting that the men are missing a substantial amount of what she's saying.

Why? Because her stylish professional outfit includes a low neckline and cleavage. And among the thousands of men and women I have interviewed and surveyed over the years, I have found no subject more universally misunderstood than what a man thinks when he sees a woman overtly showing a good figure.

Women tend to think, *I want to feel good about myself, look stylish, make a good impression.* When we hear someone caution us that we should watch what we wear around men, we may have the indignant thought, *It's none of his business what I'm wearing. He shouldn't be looking.*

But a man thinks, *She wants me to look at her body. No, look at her face. Is she flirting with me? Shoot, what did she just say about the loan failure rate? I missed it.*

When I first interviewed a few trusted Christian male friends for the novel that eventually led to this research, this is the subject that woke me up to how much I didn't know about men. Ironically, the scene that opened my eyes, that I was describing for the men, was a business situation. I had placed my male character, Doug, in a conference room listening to whiteboard presentations from a series of executives, one of whom was a woman. I described her as all business, but also as very attractive and wearing a suit or blouse that showed off her figure in some way—a low-cut shirt or a tight skirt. Then I asked each man I interviewed, "If you were in Doug's place, what would be going through your mind as the female executive made her presentation?" I was stunned to hear:

"Great body... Stop it! What am I thinking?"

"I feel an instant tightening in my gut."

"I'll bet she's using those curves to sell this deal."

"Look at her face, look at her face, look at her face..."

"I wonder what's under that nice suit? Stop it. Concentrate on the presentation."

I was unnerved to hear these comments and others, especially from happily married, godly men who were respectful of women. Since that time, I've heard similar reactions from thousands of men and realized that when it comes to the ways talented women may unknowingly undermine men's perception of them, this one is near the top of the list. Why? Because of the disproportionate impact it has on a man's thoughts and how drastically it affects the way the woman is perceived. And yet, in most instances, the woman has no idea what is really going on inside the minds of the men around her.

The subject of a man's visual nature can be awkward and sensitive to discuss. It may also engender some perplexed questions ("Is this outfit 'overtly showing my figure,' or is it just attractive?") and even stronger reactions. Some women just shrug and say, "What's the big deal?" Others find it offensive. Many women are quite cautious in how they present themselves, while others simply don't realize their choices are setting up the men they encounter for a real struggle. Still other women are highly attuned to this issue but need help as they try to discuss it with co-workers, interns, and those they mentor.

Regardless of whether or not we agree with, dislike, or even comprehend certain commonly held male perceptions in this area, it is definitely in our best interest not to be in the dark about them. More fundamentally, we are admonished, as the apostle Paul says in Philippians, to look "not only to [our] own interests, but also to the interests of others."

As you will see, how we present ourselves as women very definitely falls into that category. The data in this chapter will help you get up to speed on a reality that men think we already know but that, in fact, many women don't.

WHAT A WOMAN INTENDS, WHAT A MAN SEES

You may have heard more than once that "men are visual"—but do you know what that actually means? According to brain scientists and researchers such as Michael Gurian, some percent of women (perhaps as high as 25 percent) are visual in a similar way to men.[1] If you're in that category, you are more likely to instinctively understand men's reactions. The other 75 percent of women who aren't that visual have very little concept of how men see them.

Men and women both have individual quirks of our biological wiring that we'd rather not have: temptations, frustrations, impulses, desires. Often, these are parts of our makeup that we would love to be able to just turn off. For example, when I'm on a diet I would love to switch off the quirk in my wiring that becomes utterly attuned to the chocolate cake on the dessert cart when I'm at a restaurant. Or at someone's house for dinner. Or in the grocery store... As someone who has to watch my weight, it's frustrating to have no "off switch" for my sweet tooth. Instead, I have to work to ignore it and manage that temptation.

Men's visual wiring presents a similar temptation that men say they often don't want and wish they could turn off—including in a business setting. Their brain is biologically predisposed to take in appealing images, such as images of an appealing woman. If that woman is dressing in a way that emphasizes her assets, that fact is not only noticed but often begins a train of thought that most men in Work World, especially godly men, would not want.

A man's visual nature doesn't have an off switch any more than my sweet tooth. Fortunately, however, the Bible makes clear that there is a difference between being tempted and being in sin (see Hebrews 4:15). Just as I am incredibly aware of the chocolate cake across the room and must work to ignore it, a man must make an effort of his will to counter a visual distraction and stop his train of thought. So while many men I spoke with do make that effort (as opposed to those who clearly preferred the visual thrills), they would dearly love to *not* have to deal with the situation to begin with.

> *A man's visual nature doesn't have an off switch. They would far rather not have to deal with the situation.*

Most men I talked to are puzzled as to why women wouldn't want to avoid the situation also. Why, they wonder, would a skilled, professional woman (especially a godly woman) dress in a way that causes men to be distracted, struggle to shut down temptation, and miss what she's saying? The answer, of course, is that most women have no intention of causing that sort of a mental struggle, and they don't realize they're doing so.

To test the difference in men's and women's perceptions in this area, I asked men what they would think if they saw a woman dressing in a way that emphasized or showed off her figure in some way, such as a low-cut top or a tight skirt. Then I asked white-collar women, who said they sometimes dressed that way, what was going through their minds. The starkly differing results may surprise you:

- Seventy-six percent of the men felt the woman wanted the men around her to look at her body.
- Yet only 23 percent of the women actually wanted that.

In other words, three out of four such women said that was not what they were thinking at all!

One man I interviewed worked alongside many women. When I asked him if he ever saw them do things that in his opinion sabotaged their success, he paused. Then he proceeded gingerly:

Women more than men have some subtle ways of maybe not looking as professional. [Looking uncomfortable, he gestured to his shirt.] Like a woman's shirt that is unbuttoned too low. Or is tight. You know what I'm saying? I think a woman in a business situation that is dressed simply and not trying to call attention to herself is received better. A guy can relax in that situation a little more than if...well, if the lady is trying to call attention to herself. And, subconsciously, I'm sorry, but the message comes across. She's looking for that attention. It can be really distracting.

Most of us work hard at making a good impression in the workplace. The problem isn't that we don't know it is important. The problem is we often don't realize when the visual impression we are making differs from the one we intend.

Based on the seven nationally representative surveys I've commissioned over the years for my books, I can almost guarantee that the professional woman who puts on a figure-framing crossover blouse under her suit isn't "looking for attention" (at least, the overtly sexual attention he assumes) or "trying to send a message." But that is how almost every man perceives it. To understand why, let's look at the visual wiring of men and the ways in which it differs from the average woman's physiological makeup.

THE VERY VISUAL MALE BRAIN

To put it simply, the average man's brain structure and chemical mix make it impossible for him not to be visually oriented, especially toward stimuli he perceives as sexual. Of course, God intended this to be a good thing, since the only sexual image a man was ever supposed to see was of his wife. Yet in today's world, men and women are presented with temptations we were never supposed to face.

Let's take a deep breath and look at a few truths about the biology of the male brain.

A man's brain is more visually oriented. Neuroscientists consistently find that more areas of the male brain are devoted to visual-spatial processing than in the female brain.[2]

By contrast, more areas of the female brain are devoted to verbal and emotional processing. Where a woman's brain predisposes her to experience the world more relationally, a man's brain predisposes him to experience the world much more visually. Researchers at the University of California, Vanderbilt University, and the Veterans Affairs Medical Center in Minneapolis found that even in a neutral rest state, men's brains are much more attuned to external visual stimuli, and women's brains more attuned to internal sensory stimuli.[3]

Men are more highly attuned to stimuli they perceive as sexual. Testosterone increases the assertiveness of a person's sex drive, which is why men (with more testosterone) tend to have a greater desire to initiate or pursue sex. But as Michael Gurian describes in *What Could He Be Thinking?* men's visual nature, combined with more testosterone, combined with more vasopressin and dopamine (brain chemicals that affect memory, sexual bonding, and emotions), also make men far more visually aware of sexual stimuli and far more likely to perceive certain stimuli as sexual in the first place.[4]

In particular, men are far more likely to automatically perceive the sight of an attractive person of the opposite sex as sexual. A group of scientists from Massachusetts General Hospital, Harvard Medical School, and Massachusetts Institute of Technology found through functional MRI scans (fMRIs) that men's brains are affected at a very primal level when they look at pictures of women they perceive as attractive.[5]

As ABC's John Stossel put it when he reported on this study in 2002, "The same part of the brain [the nucleus accumbens] lights up when a young man sees a picture of a beautiful woman as when a hungry person sees food, or a gambler eyes cash, or a drug addict sees a fix."[6]

The gut reaction: *I want that!*

Men's initial reactions are stronger, more visceral, and more automatic. Thus, far more than with women, a man who encounters visual stimuli that he perceives as sexual has an automatic tendency to become mentally aroused. While men can choose what they do from that point forward, their initial response is often purely biological, rather than voluntary. David M. Buss, a professor of psychology at the University of Texas at Austin, says, "Telling men not to become aroused by signs of beauty, youth, and health is like telling them not to experience sugar as sweet."[7]

And men simply have stronger biological responses to such stimuli than women. According to a study by Emory University researchers published in the professional journal *Nature Neuroscience,* when men and women see sexual stimuli, a man's amygdala, which regulates emotion and aggression, and hypothalamus, which primes a hormonal response, are more strongly activated.[8]

Men also store and recall visual sexual stimuli very differently than women. First, as noted by Dr. Richard M. Restak, a professor of neurology at George Washington Hospital University School of Medicine, visual experiences are more likely than any other sensory input to be retained in memory.[9] And men experience the world much more visually in the first place. Finally, remembering that the male amygdala is much larger and more active, consider how Dr. Walt and Barb Larimore's book *His Brain, Her Brain* explains how our memory treats sexually attractive images:

> The amygdala amplifies memories which are pleasant.... It communicates to the hippocampus which memories need to be locked in place.... In men, these areas of the limbic system are far better connected to the spinal cord [the instinctive, visceral center] than they are to the cortex [the thinking center].[10]

In other words, when men or women see or remember a sexually attractive member of the opposite sex, women are more likely to think, *He's an attractive man* (a more thought-oriented response), where men are more likely to feel a gut-level sense of desire that they then have to bring under their intellectual control: *Stop it. Look at her face.* But since the more gut-level responses are far more likely to be tied to memory, by the time the man's intellect kicks in, the visual image is likely stamped into his brain.

And the next challenge is that those memories resurface. Joseph LeDoux, a neuroscientist at the Center for Neural Science at New York University, was the first to identify a sort of shortcut from the hypothalamus to the amygdala for certain memories that entirely bypasses the thinking centers of the brain. In effect, the amygdala acts as a kind of repository for gut-level impressions and memories tied to gut-level responses. And those memories bypass the thinking centers to involuntarily pop up again in a person's mind.[11]

Where a woman (more oriented toward processing emotion) is more likely to have emotional pop-up memories, men are more likely to have visual pop-up memories: an image suddenly replays in his mind. At that point, the man's thinking and will generally kick in, and he can choose what to do from then on.

WHAT *VISUAL* MEANS IN PRACTICE

So what does this mean in terms of how men visually experience day-to-day life, including in the workplace? As you read—especially if you are disturbed by these realities—remember that most men dislike this pattern of temptation as much as we do. Many men are eager for women to understand how it happens so as to stop triggering it!

Workplace Reality 1: Men can't *not* notice

In my research, women's most fundamental misconception about men's visual nature is the notion that men can somehow turn off their initial sexual awareness and attraction. Based on responses in my interviews and surveys, it appears that if a man is heterosexual, he can't *not* notice. Now, a man can choose whether or not to *look*, and he can make decisions about how he will handle the situation once he notices. But the fact is there is an involuntary component to his initial awareness and attraction. Men can't just turn off their visual nature.

Now, you and I might think, *It's none of a man's business what I'm wearing or what I look like!* But what we may not realize is, once we select clothes that are revealing (even if *we* don't think of them that way), we have made them a man's business.

There is a great deal of evidence for this, including from one of the surveys I conducted for my book *For Women Only*. It's important to note that this survey essentially provided a non-business-setting control group of men who weren't affected by the inherent wariness of answering business-related questions. Here's the situation I painted for male survey takers:

Imagine you are sitting alone in a train station and a woman with a great body walks in and stands in a nearby line. What is your reaction to the woman? (Choose one answer.)

a. I openly stare at her.	4%
b. I'm drawn to look at her, and I sneak a peek or glance at her from the corner of my eye.	76%
c. It is impossible not to be aware that she is there, but I try to stop myself from looking.	18%
d. Nothing happens; it doesn't affect me.	2%

0%   50%   100%

As you can see, nearly all the men put their response to an eye-catching woman in the "can't not be attracted" categories.

It is hard for us as women to understand exactly what such a visual orientation is like. This example can help. Start by looking at the letters in this box—*but whatever you do, don't read the words:*

> ## DON'T READ THIS

Were you able to look at the letters, but not read the words?

It's impossible, right? Your brain reads the words before you can stop it, *even if you are trying not to.* That is what it is like for a man when, for example, an attractive woman with a figure-hugging outfit knocks on his office door, asking whether the budget report is ready for review. His brain reads, *"Great body,"* before his intellect can override his biology.

Many men told me they are frustrated by having to face this at work (and elsewhere!). One man explained, "Women need to understand: we don't fundamentally change how we see certain things just because we are at work instead of somewhere else. I'd rather not have noticed that my colleague is wearing a black bra this morning underneath her blouse, but there's nothing I can do about that now. All I can do is to try to keep out of her way."

I'll examine the ramifications of this biological wiring shortly. But in the meantime, let's look at this critical caveat.

IF THE WOMAN'S FIGURE ISN'T EMPHASIZED, A MAN'S INVOLUNTARY SEXUAL RESPONSE ISN'T TRIGGERED.

Fortunately, a woman can be very attractive—and very attractively dressed—and yet trigger none of this involuntary sexual response in a man. The key question is whether her clothing choices draw overt attention to her body or not. (For example, a top that shows any cleavage, a body-hugging outfit, or a short skirt.) Now, that doesn't mean that a man can't choose to stir up his visual nature, regardless of how careful the woman is, but that is an entirely different discussion beyond her control (and beyond the scope of this book).

Workplace Reality 2: Images can pop up in men's minds

One of the most perplexing elements of a man's visual nature, maybe because we have no equivalent to it, is that the appealing and sexual images a man sees can be stored in his brain like picture files stored on a computer. These images then can pop up in his mind without warning. (They can also be called up at will.)

Most of us know what it's like to have thoughts and feelings pop up in our minds: concerns, worries, and "what if" scenarios that arise seemingly out of nowhere. That is very similar to how men describe their visual memories, only what pops up is equivalent to either a picture or a live-action video. A man may be sitting at his desk, reviewing the latest marketing plan, when suddenly the screen of his mind replays a sensual scene from a movie he saw last week. Or he can be in a long meeting about how to cut fuel costs, but when his attractive female colleague stands up to work some numbers at the whiteboard, it suddenly triggers a recollection of what she looked like last week in that short, tight skirt.

Again, a man can push down these unwanted visual memories by distraction or force of will, just as women can with emotional pop-ups. But to do so, he has to make it a choice.

Most men have had years of practice at managing their reaction along a spectrum of possible choices. They can't entirely avoid the temptation, but the more they choose to wrench their thoughts away and think about something else, the less frequently such thoughts intrude over the long run.

WORKPLACE IMPLICATIONS FOR WOMEN

The men I surveyed described four workplace outcomes—none of them positive—that derive directly from a woman dressing in a way that men consider too revealing.

Negative Outcome 1: He's missing some of what she's saying

The ramification of most concern to professional women is the distraction factor. A man is trying so hard to push down his awareness of an appealing image (*Look at her face*) that he's distracted from the task at hand and missing some of what the woman is saying.

One survey taker said a woman can undermine herself if she "dresses in a way that distracts her male workers. Not that she intends for this to happen—it's just a natural reaction that lowers her perceived effectiveness."

> *The man is trying so hard to not notice that he's distracted and missing some of what the woman is saying.*

One sales director for a $1 billion company provided an example of how this plays out:

I have a twenty-something saleswoman on my sales team. She's extremely competent, extremely attractive, and has a tendency to wear high-fashion, *Sex and the City*–type outfits. On one sales call, I accompanied her for our first presentation to the customer, a forty-something guy. I thought she did a phenomenal job, but a few days later, in a different meeting with that customer, I realized this guy didn't remember a thing from the first meeting about our product or our corporate capabilities. A week later I had a male sales rep make the exact same presentation as the woman had—and the customer had a laundry list of questions throughout the meeting. It was the same presentation and he didn't remember a thing.

Two-thirds of the men I surveyed—and nearly every man I interviewed—agreed there would be a distraction factor. Take a look at the survey results to the scenario I created:

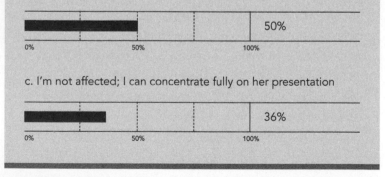

Imagine you are in a business meeting, and a woman with a great body stands up to give a presentation. She is all business, but she is wearing a suit and blouse that show off her figure in some way (for example, a low-cut blouse or tight skirt). Which answer below most closely describes the likely impact of that on your ability to concentrate on her presentation? (Choose one answer.)

a. I'm instinctively drawn to look at her body, and sneak in peeks when she won't notice—so I'm missing quite a bit of what she says

14%

0%   50%   100%

b. I try to concentrate, but I'm distracted from trying to look at her face and not her body—so I miss some of what she says

50%

0%   50%   100%

c. I'm not affected; I can concentrate fully on her presentation

36%

0%   50%   100%

Two out of three men said they would miss either "quite a bit" or "some" of what the woman was saying. Only one-third said they would be able to concentrate fully on her presentation. And nearly every man to whom I have shown this has expressed amused skepticism about the latter number.

One man chuckled, pointed to the 36 percent "I'm not affected" number, and said, "That is the 'liar, liar, pants on fire' cohort."

"HER CLEAVAGE IS TALKING"

A clever commercial during the 2008 Super Bowl, for Tide to Go stain remover, caught the attention of a male friend with whom Jeff and I were watching the game. The ad showed a job interviewee with a noticeable stain on his shirt. As he talked to the manager across the desk, the stain grew a big pair of lips and began to talk in nonsense words, making it impossible for the manager (and TV viewer) to concentrate on what the interviewee was saying.

Our friend knew I was researching the effect of visual images on men. He turned to me and pointed at the television. "That is exactly what it is like when a woman's outfit shows cleavage," he said. "It's like her cleavage is talking. And you aren't able to concentrate on a word she's saying."

In an out-of-town interview a few weeks later, a Christian executive brought up the exact same commercial:

> It's not just cleavage. If she's attractive, it is any emphasis to her figure, even if it's a tattoo. It is hard to concentrate when the tattoo is peeking out. I had one lady working for me who was incredibly bright and personable. During a wilder part of her life, she had gotten a tattoo. I didn't even know it was there until she came in one day wearing something more summery. You start wondering, *How low does that go?*

This man agreed that men's visual nature can be easily distracted by other things that aren't sexual at all. As he said, "There's a thing among some of my younger staff members about facial piercings. Like nose studs. But it is really hard to take someone seriously when their nose is blinking at you."

THE VISUAL EXPERIMENT

Once I began to hear all this, I wanted to see if I could estimate the degree of the actual distraction factor. While re-creating and testing my survey question in a live environment would have taken more time and resources than I had left, I could at least examine the impact of a short video clip and assume the actual impact would be greater in a real-world situation.

Working with my survey designer, research assistants, and a team of studio and online specialists, I created two ninety-second videos of an attractive businesswoman wearing a suit and presenting "the four top customer suggestions" for a fictitious retail-clothing company. The presenter introduces herself as Laurie Boss, director of customer service. The only difference between the two videos is that in one she wears her crossover top low to show her cleavage, and in the other she wears it high, eliminating cleavage.

We then created a short survey about the content of the presentation. Without knowing what was being tested, 409 men took this survey online, randomly seeing one of the two videos.

The results? There was a clear difference in what they absorbed and retained. The percentage of men who remembered her four points dropped by 25 percent if they saw the more revealing version of the video. Where 64 percent of men who saw the more conservative video remembered her four points, only 48 percent of those who saw the more revealing version did.

Given the artificial distance imposed by watching a short video online, and the memory-jogging assistance of answering multiple questions about it immediately afterward, the distraction factor would almost certainly be higher in a real-life environment. In fact, at the end of the survey for the more revealing video, several men commented that without the survey questions, they wouldn't have recalled much at all about what Laurie Boss presented. As one described it, "If I hadn't taken the survey afterward, I wouldn't have remembered anything she said. But tomorrow and a week from now, I would still remember her cleavage."

> *The percentage of men who remembered her four points dropped by 25 percent if they saw cleavage.*

Overall, I asked the men who had seen that version of the video two totally open-ended questions about their impression of "Laurie Boss" and what she could have done to improve her customer-service presentation. Nearly six in ten volunteered that the most important adjustment would not be adding visual aids, speaking more slowly, or adding more quotes from customers: they said she should change her top. Several of their comments essentially summarize the male dilemma:

- "I had to avoid looking at the woman's cleavage to better focus on what she was saying."
- "Her top was too revealing, therefore very distracting, so it took a lot of concentration to determine what she was talking about."
- "The speaker's outfit was distracting. A more conservative outfit would assist male viewers to focus more on the information being relayed."
- "Too much cleavage in the announcer. Draws attention away from presentation. I took notes and therefore could listen better without looking."

Negative Outcome 2: He usually thinks the woman wants to be viewed sexually

The awkward and sobering reality is that men and women have entirely different views on why a woman would dress in a way that shows off her figure. My survey and interviews demonstrate that the large majority of women are not trying to attract sexual attention or fantasizing. But depending on how revealing the clothing is, and how attractive the woman is, the men often find that difficult to believe. Because men are so visually attuned and sexually aware, they have a tendency to assume women are too. They assume a woman who shows her figure knows, in the words of many men surveyed, "exactly what she is doing."

While a few of the white-collar women I surveyed did confess to wanting to manipulate male colleagues for business advantage—or to wanting male colleagues to sexually fantasize about them—the vast majority of women who occasionally show off their figure aren't thinking about that at all. In fact, most women are horrified that men would think that they are.

Here are the stark differences between how men and women perceive clothing that overtly emphasizes a woman's figure in some way. As we saw at the opening of this chapter, three of four men think the woman "wants the men around her to look at her body." Seventy percent felt the woman was showing off her body in order to create an advantage, when only 16 percent of women said that was their intent! Perhaps even more damaging, 67 percent of men said that a woman who dresses to show her figure "does understand how she's being perceived—and doesn't care."

By contrast, the large majority of white-collar women who did dress that way said their primary motivation was none of those reasons: 89 percent said they simply wanted to look good and wear what is in style.

Men have a hard time believing that this is the case, but others say this explains something that had previously confused them about women's intentions. One young man told me, "We have five men and one woman on our project team, and the woman is really attractive. She wears these suits with short skirts. She's a happy newlywed, and I've often wondered why she would want to tempt all these other guys to fantasize about her. It helps to know she's just clueless!"

Negative Outcome 3: He may view the woman with less respect

Given the common male assumption that women wear figure-showing outfits to purposefully create sexual thoughts, manipulate male colleagues, or create a business advantage, it is not surprising that some men view such women with less respect. I heard this most commonly from men who were meeting the woman on a limited basis (for example, an infrequent sales meeting or one-time project), or among those who felt a female colleague regularly dressed that way and wasn't a top performer. The more regularly a man worked with a female colleague, the more he respected her for her business performance, regardless of what she wore. He might still be equally *distracted* by her dress but was less likely to think less of her because of it.

> *The more regularly a man worked with a female colleague, the more he respected her for her business performance, regardless of what she wore. He might still be equally distracted by her dress but was less likely to think less of her because of it.*

But in situations where the man either didn't know the woman well or didn't yet view her as a top performer, men told me they tended to view her with less respect simply because of her dress. One survey taker said a key action that undermined men's perception of women was when a woman would "[dress] inappropriately for the business, but believ[e] she will still be taken seriously during important meetings."

"THEY'LL INVITE YOU BACK, BUT THEY WON'T TAKE YOU SERIOUSLY"

Mark, a well-known executive and entrepreneur, gave an example that seemed representative:

> I had a meeting yesterday with some senior people who are looking for us to make an investment and talk about a strategic partnership. They had their COO with them, who had been a senior banker for [a major global bank] with some global responsibilities. She's sitting across the table from me, leaning in, and I'm trying not to see her bra. I'm trying to figure out: *Is she trying to show me her breasts, or is she, like, clueless here?* I'm trying to have a conversation with her, and I don't even remember what she was talking about. Someone needs to get a hold of her and say, "Look, they'll invite you back, but they won't take you seriously." It's like I tell my daughters: You don't have to show your figure for guys to know you've got a good figure. They get it! You don't have to wear that outfit for guys to notice.

"THAT DOESN'T BELONG IN THE WORKPLACE"

The men I spoke with believe that "sexy" or revealing attire (including clothes women would not perceive that way) belongs exclusively in one's personal life. They think the whole point of such attire is to be eye-catching. Men viewed such dress as not relevant or appropriate for the workplace, and as actually distracting from work. As a result, they view this issue as they would any other example of bringing Personal World rules into Work World: the woman is seen as less than business savvy, even immaturely trying to create a business advantage by making the meeting about sexual attraction.

Look at how this senior executive clearly perceived it: "It creates a barrier immediately if a woman comes into a meeting showing cleavage. A woman has to get to the point where she realizes this isn't about sex, it's about business. Showing cleavage won't necessarily kill the deal, but it absolutely makes me question her judgment."

> When he sees cleavage, he automatically assumes the woman is immaturely trying to create an advantage by making the meeting about sex.

"SHE'S CLUELESS"

On the broader survey, just 39 percent of men realized what is often the truth: a woman who dresses revealingly "must not understand how she's being perceived." The realization that a woman was clueless about this also led them to respect her less, professionally.

One business owner I know attended a highly touted all-day corporate conference and described his reaction to one female speaker:

She was probably forty years old, very attractive and dynamic—but wearing this top that sort of gaped and showed her breasts. I ran into her after her talk and she was telling me how she had spent ten thousand dollars on these high-level New York speaking coaches. And the whole time she's explaining this, these perfect golden breasts are staring at me. Honestly, I felt sorry for her. I'm thinking, *You just spent ten thousand dollars on learning how to be a better public speaker, and you just blew it all*—because I doubt the men were really listening to what she was saying. And she could have been such a dynamite speaker.

EITHER GOOD OR BAD PERCEPTIONS CAN BECOME THE DEFAULT

Aidan, the global consulting partner mentioned earlier, is one of the top partners in his firm in terms of mentoring and promoting women, so he was eager to pass this thought along:

> We as men don't just leave this [visual nature] in the parking lot.... Do you want the guy at work, when he thinks of you, to picture your legs, or picture your point of view? I think most women I know, I would put in one group or the other. You can be very attractive and that isn't a problem for a guy as long as everything is covered up and not too close-fitting. If I see an attractive woman being careful about it, the mental conclusion is that she's going to rely on her point of view instead of on her looks. But if I meet someone at work with a trendy, short skirt or close-fitting clothes, I know she must know that, so she's relying on her body and the attraction factor to work in her favor.

Negative Outcome 4: This puts men who want to respect women in an awkward situation

Most men I spoke with want to be respectful of women. They don't want the distraction or temptation that jumps to their minds, especially with a female colleague they like and respect. But when a woman colleague dresses in a revealing way, they can't easily avoid the situation without also avoiding that colleague, which was the choice some of them felt forced to make. As a result, ironically, this dilemma is most challenging and demoralizing for the men who care the most about honoring and respecting the women they work with. (Those who don't care as much shrug and say, essentially, "If she wants to show it off, I'll enjoy the show.")

> *Ironically, this dilemma is most challenging for men who care the most about respecting women.*

SO WHAT'S A WOMAN TO DO?

Ask any woman: fashion trends seem to keep pushing women toward more provocative styles—tighter clothes, shorter skirts, and more revealing necklines. No wonder that even the most skilled among us may unintentionally dress in a manner that reduces our effectiveness or respect in the eyes of our male colleagues. I realize with some embarrassment that there were quite a few times I did that in the years before I learned this truth. If that applies to you as well, extend yourself some mercy for your lack of awareness and simply resolve to move forward well. If this applies not to you but to women you mentor or care about in the workplace, perhaps the release of this research provides you with a good (and less awkward) excuse to bring it up and open a line of discussion.

Thankfully, more than any other subject in this book, working wisely in light of men's visual orientation lends itself to a simple solution. The visual distraction factor is triggered when a woman dresses in a way that overtly emphasizes or calls attention to her figure, so when she doesn't dress that way, the distraction and temptation response isn't triggered. Furthermore, as Douglass, the corporate sponsorship executive I introduced earlier, reminds us:

A woman can be extremely attractive, but if she's not showing skin or wearing really form-fitting clothes, the issue doesn't come up. She's just…attractive. Women have the ability to be completely beautiful and completely appropriate.

The practical challenge, as we've seen, is that there is a clear disconnect between what women and men feel is appropriate. Several times I have stood with a man I know at a busy pedestrian area, business district, or coffee shop and asked him to point out women dressed in a way that would distract male colleagues. I was surprised at some of the choices. I'll bet that the women in question would have been surprised as well.

This disconnect was evident on the survey too. Just 4 percent and 22 percent of women, respectively, said they "frequently" or "sometimes" wore work outfits that emphasized their figure; men seemed to think that the visual dilemma occurred a lot more often.

Among men with female colleagues who don't have a strict workplace uniform, 58 percent said they see a female associate dressing in a way they find distracting at least once a week. Twelve percent said they see examples of that "every day, multiple times a day."

LOOKING AT THE SPECIFICS

In general, the younger and more attractive a woman is, the more likely this is to be an issue and, therefore, the more cautious she may want to be. (Over time, my website, www.ForWomenOnly Workplace.com, will include examples of attire that many women may think of as professional, but which men tell me is still likely to cause a problem.) In general, here is what one businessman said about the factors that tend to trigger the problem:

Curves, bare skin, and, frankly, the sight of whatever is supposed to be covered—that is what a man's eyes will be drawn to. A tight outfit, a short skirt, a bra strap showing, low-cut pants in the back where you can see the top of whatever she is wearing underneath if she leans over a bit—any one of those things. And cleavage. Breasts are always distracting. It is so frustrating when I see in the morning that my one female colleague is wearing a button-down shirt, because she regularly has those types of shirts unbuttoned one button too low, and where it gapes or she turns sideways you can see everything. I try to avoid looking, but I cannot put my hand up and go like this [he raised his hand as if to block his view of her chest] when I am talking to her. And of course, I cannot tell her about her top. I think she trusts me, but no guy can ever talk about this with a woman, unless she's his sister or something.

At several corporate and ministry workplace events, I asked organizers to collect anonymous input on this issue beforehand from men. This is a practice worth considering for any workplace seminar for women on this topic, since the results raised quite a few specifics. (One example: "Tell the women to remember that men are taller than they are. The blouse may look fine straight on in the mirror, but think about what it will look like if someone is six inches taller and looking down.")

HELPING OTHER WOMEN UNDERSTAND

As noted early on, some readers of this book may be in a position where they want to—or have to—pass some of this information on to female colleagues or subordinates. When I interviewed one senior female partner at a major consulting firm, she told me the men in her practice asked her several times to address this issue with specific women. These women frequently went on client calls dressed in ways the men felt were counterproductive. Yet the men didn't feel they could bring it up: they simply wanted it corrected before it caused client problems. The senior female partner was one of the top rainmakers for that firm and way too busy to take on this extra task. Moreover, she said she resented the fact that just because she was a woman, she was expected to "be a sort of baby-sitter to women who should know better." Because she was so busy, and didn't know how to address the issue in a nonoffensive way, she never followed up.

I know from experience that making other women aware of this issue can be awkward. It helps to get the other person's permission in advance. For example, you might say, "I have something a bit awkward that I want to ask you about, but it's something you might find important because it could affect how you may be perceived. Would you mind if I raised it with you?"

Another female executive I know said she is always getting "stuck" with having this conversation because she's one of the most senior women in her company and no man feels able to raise the subject with the women in question. The men go to my friend, and my friend has to raise this as part of her job. She said this approach is most effective:

> It starts with ensuring you are respectful and discreet.
> You need to do it in such a way that no one else knows
> the conversation is happening. I have had to do this
> multiple times. I ask the woman to come into my office,
> close the door, and I say, "This is really awkward, but I
> have something I need to talk to you about—let me just
> blurt this out, and we can clean it up later. I just have
> to address what you're wearing, and want to walk you
> through why it probably isn't the best choice for this work
> environment, or this meeting. It's both for your sake and
> the company's reputation. I'm so sorry, but I just have to
> bring this up."

"How do you explain the actual issue to the woman, though?" I asked. "If she's confused, or doesn't understand why this is an issue, or if she's offended?"

I ask her, "When you do this meeting, what do you want to be remembered for?"

She will almost always say, "My presentation! I've got the stats, I've been working hard on this, and now it's time to present it."

I then say, "Okay, so if you want to be remembered for the presentation, you do everything you can to ensure that is the focal point, and you do everything you can to minimize any possible distractions, right? You think ahead of time about avoiding distractions—you silence your cell phone, for example, or close the conference room door so people don't get distracted by outside noise. We often don't realize it, but it works the same way with what we're wearing. If you want them to remember your presentation and not your feather hoop earrings or red stilettos, don't wear them. And if you want them to remember your two main points and not your cleavage, then you should probably change before the meeting."

Sometimes I jokingly say, "You just happen to have a figure that I would kill for, so you may have to think more specifically about how to make it a nonissue, so the guys can concentrate on what you're saying."

A TOOL TO HELP YOU

Finally, as an aid for any managers, workers, or human-resource people who want to address this with their female employees or colleagues, I'll be creating tools that might help, including a short presentation that summarizes the findings discussed in this chapter, in particular the results of the video experiment showing the distraction factor. Over time, you will find those resources on www.ForWomenOnlyWorkplace.com.

The good news is this: in my workplace talks, this uncomfortable subject ends up being one of the most empowering for women to learn—because it is the easiest to do something about. Like all the other subjects covered in this book, the key is to have our eyes opened.

CHAPTER 8

"The Most Important Thing"

Men's Top Advice for Women in the Workplace

After reading a few hundred pages about men's perceptions, you might be tempted to assume that men expect you to set aside who you are and become "like a man" in the workplace. But that is not the case at all. When I asked an entirely open-ended question about the single most important piece of advice men would offer women in the workplace, one resounding theme emerged:

Be competent and confident in who you are. You are respected and we're cheering you on.

Of all the insights I heard from men, this one stands out above the rest, and I would like to highlight it as we arrive at the final chapters of this book.

THE FINAL QUESTION

As you know by now, I had asked the men two dozen multiple-choice survey questions on a host of subjects, as well as the core question about whether (and how) they saw talented women unintentionally shoot themselves in the foot. As the final question on the survey, I gave the survey takers a blank field in which they could write as much or as little as they liked, and asked this question: "Finally, if you could give one piece of advice to women in the workplace, what is the one most important thing you would say to them?"

Nearly everyone responded, and fully half of the men essentially gave answers like these:

1. Just be yourself and confident in who you are.
2. Be competent, and you'll do well.
3. You're respected; keep up the great work.

Many gave a combination of all three.

Think about this. Faced with a blank space for them to say anything at all, 51 percent of the men chose to offer one or more of those three very encouraging messages as their "most important advice."[1] I hope you find that as astonishing—and as reassuring—as I do.

> *The fact that 51 percent said their top advice was, "Be competent, be yourself, and keep up the great work," is astonishing, when they had a blank space and could say anything at all.*

Let's look briefly at these three top encouragements from men.[2]

"BE YOURSELF; BE CONFIDENT IN WHO YOU ARE"

I was personally very encouraged that so many men were in effect pleading with women to embrace, not suppress, the unique way God has designed us as women. In fact, men said the other approach—trying to become who we're not—usually backfired because they could tell a woman wasn't being genuine. This inauthenticity tended to create distrust in interactions.

Matthew, the North American sales manager for a medical equipment supplier, described it this way:

I think sometimes the perceived need to survive takes over the personality or the natural disposition of some people. And my personal impression is that the effect is far more pronounced in women than it is in men. We had several thousand female sales reps at [his last company] and I often saw an overcompensation among women who felt like they had to change who they were in order to be successful. And that overcompensation often seemed to impact those characteristics that were decidedly female. But you can see strong female leaders who haven't done that—and haven't needed to. Margaret Thatcher was someone with the intellectual discipline and acumen to best any man in the room. She could be tough, but she maintained that characteristic that is distinctly female.

He paused for a moment and then said,

You know what? I don't know that my favorable impression has anything to do, really, with a woman maintaining feminine qualities, as much as with the fact that she is not changing who she naturally is. With Margaret Thatcher, you got the impression of honesty. Something that was not compromised. A truth in her speech and in her demeanor that said, "Look, I am tough, but I am also square with who I am."

People who change are not being themselves. It is like they are not in their own skin. That is not viewed well. Generally, people prefer to work with those who are genuine. There are a lot of people that would want to meet with a female account executive over a male account executive any day, because they appreciate their style. You don't want to lose that.

One partner in a major New York law firm told me,

> Sometimes I have seen a woman try to overcompensate for
> the perception that she as a woman might not be a
> take-charge person. But by overcompensating she loses the
> natural strengths she has. She loses the ability to build a
> team, or lead a team in a less aggressive way, and she
> becomes almost obnoxious. A few days ago, I was sitting
> down with a team of lawyers from a potential M&A deal,
> led by a female partner. She was highly competent, and
> she knew what she was talking about, but she sounded and
> carried herself like a man. And I thought, *Whoa! I wonder*
> *what she must have gone through, to become like that.*
> Because the changes she had to force upon herself made
> her a strange person. Her body language, her coarse
> language, her tone. The words were abrasive. She was
> carrying a macho attitude like, "I'm in charge, and I want
> everyone to know it." A more overtly macho attitude, by
> the way, than most men have in a professional environ-
> ment. I would have greater respect for her if she would just
> be herself. Trying to project a different image is not
> natural, for either a woman or a man.

As I was traveling to talk to a corporate women's network, one
man cautioned, "Ironically, my female colleagues who try to 'be
like men' tend to pick the most *unattractive* attributes of men—the
hard personality traits that men dislike about each other!" One
recently retired senior executive in the newspaper industry brought
up several similar examples but then contrasted those with this
encouragement:

> I grew up in publishing, so starting in the 1970s, I have
> encountered a lot of fantastically talented women in that

industry, in the investment world, in the financial world, and in the advertising/marketing world. And the ones that endured were women who had acquired a sort of confidence, a type of wholeness about them. They were sure of themselves and sure of their identity as women and very professional. They knew their borders, they knew their boundaries, but they did well because they knew they had to interact with men on a level that was extraordinarily professional, but human, extraordinarily human.

The men I interviewed brought up this "Don't feel you have to be like a man" point so frequently that I ended up including a related question on the survey and forcing the men into a choice. Essentially, the question was this: Would you trust and respect someone more if they were being themselves, instead of trying to create a persona? Or would you trust and respect someone more if they got the job done, period, even if in the process they put on the persona of someone they clearly were not?

Even though these men had clearly shown their "results orientation" on other questions, in the end, 77 percent of the male survey takers had more respect for a person who was being authentic.

By now you might be wondering, as I did, *How can men say, "Be yourself," when they also are clearly suggesting that it might be valuable for women to change their approach in certain areas?*

One survey taker's top advice provided an answer that rang true with me and helped to clarify what they mean: "Be your *professional* self [emphasis mine]. Don't try to be a man, because the fact is, you're not."

Another said, "Be yourself but realize that people, men and women, are different. There is sometimes a need to adjust to people, whether you want to or not."

Two men I interviewed made some particularly helpful distinctions. As one put it, "When men say, 'Just be yourself,' they truly mean it—but it *doesn't* mean, 'So anything goes.' Men have all these professional expectations, right? Those rules essentially set their expected boundary for the workplace. And 'Just be yourself' essentially means, 'Within the rules, relax and be confident in who you are.'"

> "'Just be yourself' essentially means, 'Within the boundaries of the workplace, relax and be confident in who you are.'"

Another provided an excellent analogy:

> When you go to France, you are not going to be understood if you just speak louder in English. You have to speak French. This is like that. You learn to use a different language, but you don't have to be a different person.

And many men pointed out just how much is lost when someone does not leverage her natural, God-given strengths. As one survey taker advised, "Be genuine. There's no need to be like a man to succeed. When there's too much masculine energy, sometimes we lose sight of other perspectives."

"BE COMPETENT, AND YOU'LL DO WELL"

One of the key themes running through all my research is summed up in this response: "Gender is irrelevant—be competent."

When I went back through my interviews, I was struck by the fact that there were literally hundreds of quotes from men on this point. They emphasized it over and over, often returning to it several times in the same interview. I realized, in retrospect, that the men weren't sure I (or other women) would believe them or fully grasp the centrality of their belief that the modern market is largely gender blind.

While several of my chapters show that *largely* is the operative word, this perception about competence is nevertheless worth highlighting—with one very key caveat. As you have seen, part of what men view as "competence" includes the ability to fit into the rules and culture of the workplace, and all the other expectations addressed in this book. But that said, this perception was still encouraging.

Here are just a few of the survey takers' quotes on this topic (see my website for more):

- "As far as I am concerned—and I am the CEO—results are what matter. Intelligent, efficient people of either sex deserve my full and complete support. I am male, but I would never even consider paying a female less than a male for the same work. My advice therefore is to stand up and demand full equality of sexes in the workplace. Nothing less should be acceptable. Companies that cannot grasp this deserve to lose the quality female employees to more enlightened companies." (It is worth noting that this CEO has between 500 and 999 employees under him, according to the demographics given by each anonymous survey taker.)
- "Performance speaks volumes. Work on being very good at your job, then adding value beyond your job in some way (through leadership or resolving thorny problems or bringing and implementing new ideas). Solid performance as well as adding value tends to help all men and women be given greater responsibilities in time."
- "Believe in yourself! It doesn't matter whether you're a man or a woman, it's how well you do your job."

- "Just be yourself and do the best job you can do. Your performance will speak for itself."
- "I believe a confident, warm, and capable personality is respected in almost every endeavor for both men and women. The woman who tries to be one of the men by being rough or crude or tough is often thought of as someone not being true to her natural gender, and hence disagreeable. Integrity, capability, and a secure personality are what is most respected and appreciated in a woman in any position."

> "Integrity, capability, and a secure personality are what is most respected and appreciated in a woman in any position."

With all these comments in mind, one survey taker did provide an important caution:

Be yourself and work to the best of your abilities. In most situations that will be enough to enable you to have a pleasant and gainful work experience. And if it does not, then you should consider finding an environment that does allow you to be yourself and successful at the same time.

"YOU'RE RESPECTED; KEEP UP THE GREAT WORK"

Finally, a large number of the male survey takers were very personally encouraging. It was almost as if they wanted to convey to the women reading these results just how much they respected and were cheering on women in the workplace.

Even though many of the same men acknowledged that women still face certain disadvantages, the spirit behind their comments was encouraging. Here is just a random sampling of their actual comments:

- "Be confident in what you do, and let others know why what you do is important. Show that you are capable of responding to any situation in a positive manner."
- "Be professional and strong minded."
- "Be strong. Not every man will be accepting of or act appropriately around women in the workplace, but there are a lot out there who do. It will keep getting better."

> "Not every man will be accepting of or act appropriately around women in the workplace, but there are a lot out there who do. It will keep getting better."

- "Continue to be compassionate and dedicated to your professional goals without letting the opinions and preconceptions of male co-workers get in the way."
- "Do not be intimidated by some men. You are probably smarter."
- "Do not let anyone treat you as a lesser person."
- "Express your opinions. Don't be afraid to speak up!"
- "For both men and women in the workplace: You must perceive yourself as equal before anyone else will do so. Have the confidence, the dedication, and the professionalism to know that you are capable of working on

an equal level of even the highest of authorities in your field. Carry this confidence without arrogance and without a standoffish attitude."

- "Have confidence in yourself and you will exude confidence to those around you."
- "I would tell the women that they are just as capable as men and should not feel like they have to work twice as hard to be recognized."
- "Keep doing what you are doing—eventually, the men in the workplace who don't 'get it,' will."
- "Keep standing up for your rights to be paid equally with men."
- "Keep up the good work."
- "Never give up and don't believe you are inferior."
- "Strive to reach the top."
- "Take ownership of your opinions and work; never apologize for doing a good job."

MEN WANT TO BE OUR PARTNERS IN THE WORKPLACE

The bottom line for most of the men I interviewed is that despite their natural bent toward competition, they truly view women as equal partners in the workplace, working toward the shared goal of success for the organization. And they encouraged women to view things the same way. Both for the good of the company and—given an environment in which women still face unique hurdles—for the good of the woman's career. As one man put it, "All things still are not equal in the corporate world. Keep working for equal respect, but try not to alienate the ones who reach out their hands as allies."

Another said, "Some men may still be prone to perceiving you in the 'typical male' way, but women can do a lot to create how they want to be perceived. Confident and direct communication will show your level of competency and talent, regardless of gender."

> "Some men may still be prone to perceiving you in the 'typical male' way, but women can do a lot to create how they want to be perceived."

A senior executive search leader I interviewed, who had worked with many high-level female executives over the years, strongly advised women to be keenly aware of the level of partnership and relationship needed as we rise to the top. The women who have tended to succeed, he noted, are those women who marshal their strength in relationship building and are willing to focus on others, rather than just themselves. He explained,

> This is something that a lot of people—men or women—never understand. The very thing that may help a certain type of lower-ranking person fight toward the top of the ladder—like the sharp elbows and the willingness to step up on somebody else's hand—are the very things that prevent that person getting to the very top. Because the last three rungs of the ladder do not come as a result of that.
>
> You might get through a pack of managers and a pack of directors and even a pack of senior directors in that way—but to reach the highest ranks of the company, there is a high level of emotional intelligence required. In the middle of the company, it is making the numbers work; it is making the customers happy; it is a lot of metrics that measure success. At the top of the company, it is extraordinarily relational.

What ultimately creates success is being able to create beneficial relationships with shareholders, stakeholders, customers, and key employees. Companies that succeed have figured out a way to have a very, very high trust factor at the top, people at the highest levels being willing to work together and really understand each other.

Women who operate that way, he concluded, "can be very, very effective."

On a long coast-to-coast flight, I handed out thirty or forty paper surveys to businessmen on the plane. While I was tallying the results, I turned one survey over and found the man had used the space to provide this summary of what he would "most want to tell women":

Men like confidence. Men are drawn to warm personalities. Men respect competence. Men like secure women who stand above the petty "din" of the gossip and fear that can often be in the workplace. Men want *partners* to build something together [his emphasis]. The striving of competition in and out of the workplace stems from fear and hurt and insecurities on the part of both men and women. If these are done away with, the woman and man both can find their voices and rise equally according to achievement and contribution within an organization. Personally, I know the female energy within an organization adds to the richness of the environment. It would be nice to let the women know that they are noticed and appreciated, and it's not all a battle.

> *"It would be nice to let the women know that they are noticed and appreciated, and it's not all a battle."*

WHAT YOU TAKE FROM THIS RESEARCH

Throughout this book, I have emphasized that my purpose in bringing these facts to light is to equip women to make informed decisions. Each reader will take something very different away from what they have read. Some women will feel comfortable that they already understand "the male factor" in the workplace or that these things don't apply to them. Others may suspect the opposite. And our choices of what to do about it all—if anything—will vary tremendously.

Further, our choices of how to apply these truths may be significantly impacted by our faith. That is why in this Christian edition I have included a final chapter with counsel from other Christian women who have walked this road ahead of us and can share their experience and insights.

If you are compelled to learn more, exchange ideas with other women, or explore different ways to move from information to application, you can find a starting point at the website for this book, www.ForWomenOnlyWorkplace.com.

Over the last seven years of this research, I have been unexpectedly impacted by the intensity of the feelings of the men on many of these subjects—especially among those who most respect us as women and want to work with women in an effective way. For our sake as women, and for theirs as our allies and colleagues in the workplace, I hope that you will take this new knowledge seriously—and put it to work for your success, influence, and personal fulfillment on the job. I believe it presents an opportunity to address areas we may have never realized needed to be addressed, and to demonstrate that we respect not only ourselves, but those around us as well.

CHAPTER 9

Putting It in Perspective

Counsel from Experienced Christian Women

During this venture into the thoughts and feelings of men at work, perhaps you found yourself wondering, as I have, how to process and apply what you were learning in the context of your Christian beliefs. How can we use this new information not just to steward our gifts and opportunities well, but to do so in a way that honors God in the workplace?

For this Christian edition of the book, I've invited counsel from several Christian women I admire who have years of experience in navigating that question. This follows the apostle Paul's suggestion to Titus, leading the church on the island of Crete, that older women should help younger women learn how to live well.

Although these women had very different experiences and shared wisdom in several different areas, each encouraged other women to recognize several core biblical truths: in every aspect of our lives, God asks us to love our neighbor as ourselves, to look out for not just our own interests but also the interests of others, and to work as though we are working for God Himself. That includes learning additional skills (such as navigating a male-dominated workplace) in order to work with excellence. But it also includes recognizing that career advancement and efficiency can never be our primary goal.

God must always have first place in our lives, and we must be entirely at His disposal. There may even seem to be times when He asks us to let workplace efficiency and advancement take a backseat so that we can achieve something more important.

And that is the case for both men and women who want to succeed in the workplace. I have been surprised to hear that some Christian women think the Bible teaches us to routinely take a subordinate position to men in business. I don't find this in Scripture. The Bible clearly states that men and women are equal in the sight of God and at the foot of the cross. Further, God asks both men and women to "subdue" and "rule over" His creation (Genesis 1:28) and has given each of us gifts to do so. The Bible does make various specific requests of men and women within marriage, but that does not appear to carry over into the workplace.[1] Indeed, if God has given us leadership gifts, He will hold us accountable for whether we steward those gifts well.

> If God has given us leadership gifts,
> He will hold us accountable for
> whether we steward those gifts well.

With that in mind, let's take a look at some insights from the female leaders I interviewed (all names have been changed so they could speak freely). Over years of working with men, these women had come to seven key "aha" realizations and biblical reminders, and felt these were most important for women who sincerely desire to apply the findings of this book from a biblical perspective.

Insight 1: "I can ask the Creator of men how to handle them!"

One of the funniest comments I heard was from Lara, a high-powered consultant, who told me, "I realized, when I get confused, I can

ask the Creator of men how to handle them!" Lara is frequently the
only woman on her team—and is usually the leader of the team.
Here is more of what she said:

> When I read *For Women Only*, I was really struck by the
> chapter on respect. I saw how I could apply it at home, but
> it solved even more confusion at work. It explained why
> all this conflict would surface when I led teams or worked
> with men. I'd had trouble understanding why what I had
> said had changed a productive conversation into a polar-
> izing one. But then I realized: God has created me with a
> very inquisitive mind, and my approach to asking men
> questions could create a combative dynamic with them.
>
> I don't want to dishonor the men around me, but
> when time is short and you have seven people who are
> scattered or in disagreement, there are times when you
> have to ask questions. So I asked God, "What should I do
> differently?"
>
> I began to see exactly what would cause a man to feel
> like he was being backed into a corner and cause that
> combatant response. I realized that I was the one who had
> to change my approach. I saw that if we were sitting in a
> conference room, I couldn't just call these men out and
> question them.
>
> So I began prefacing my comments with "I find this
> point confusing; I'm not quite there yet. Help me under-
> stand." I was making it clear that they didn't do some-
> thing wrong, but that I needed a better understanding and
> wasn't there yet. Or at times I realized I would have to take
> it offline so they wouldn't feel that they were on display.
> Every day if I asked him, God gave me wisdom about what
> worked with that particular team.

With my next team, a totally different approach was needed because this time I was working for a set of male executives who *did* want the questions and answers ten in a row! In order to build trust and credibility, my leadership needed to be based on meeting them on their terms. Then once credibility was established, I had an opportunity for broader relationship where the men were more willing to adapt to my style as well.

Insight 2: "I represent Christ—and the impression I make reflects on Him"

Francine is a well-respected, stylish woman who has been an executive coach to both men and women for decades. She told me,

> When I'm coaching a Christian, I always try to remind him or her that whatever you do—in mannerisms, speech, or dress—you have to ask yourself one thing: "Will people see Jesus before they see me?" In many cases, you will be the only Bible that people read.

Not surprisingly, Francine believes one common area of concern is when a Christian woman is trying to be attractive but does not realize she is coming across as sexual:

> We want to be seen as beautiful women, but we have to realize that if men are looking at certain parts of our anatomy, they are not looking at our brains. I want them to be able to focus on what I'm saying and my contribution to the matter at hand. From a Christian woman's perspective, we have to err on the side of caution. We do not want to look frumpy, but we also do not want to undermine ourselves or our impression.

This goes far beyond how we look and into how we relate with other people. We are Christ's ambassadors. We are representing Him in the workplace, and not everyone in that workplace has the same worldview we do. When you look at yourself, what matters is not what you see. What matters is what the *other* person is going to see.

Insight 3: "Ultimately, I'm working for Jesus—and it is what He asks of me, and what He thinks, that matters most"

Mallory has spent her career in corporate training. She has worked in nurturing environments and in difficult ones, and the one thing she most wanted to advise younger women is this:

> Treat everything you do as if you're doing it for Jesus. That's not just your boss. If the person you're working with were Jesus, would you be talking to Him that way? Dressing like that? When I tackle something that is frustrating or I think is beneath me, and I start to wonder, "Why am I doing this?" I will literally think, *Wait a second, I'm doing this for Jesus.*
>
> Also, if you really think of it as if you were working *for* Jesus, not for man, would you start crying if someone says something petty or critical at work? When you have that vantage point, then certain things just aren't as gripping, so you won't be as thrown.

Insight 4: "How I work is just as important as what I do"

Rachel runs a large division of a well-known ministry. She is an efficiency expert with limited time, dozens of men and women working for her, and workaholic tendencies. She cautioned,

It can sometimes be excruciating to take the extra time to figure out the best approach to a person or situation—far easier to charge ahead to just get it done. But God's time is not our time. And He cares far more about who we are than what we do. In fact, I believe He cares more about *how* we do what we do than about what we actually accomplish.

As Mallory put it,

Our approach has to be about pleasing God and finding that more gratifying than pleasing ourselves or getting ahead. Would you rather make your point and make another person feel bad because he or she made you feel bad in the past? Or would you rather know that God was pleased with you?

When I asked Rachel for examples of the "how we work" principle with men, she described a management situation:

To the extent that we can disagree with or coach or direct men and yet do it in a way that they still feel respected, we'll be more productive and more in alignment with biblical principles. The marketplace tells us, "Go and direct them and get things done." But Scripture tells us to respect and love one another. And in dealing with men, if we "go and direct" them, we will not get results that will be as good as if we show them respect, challenge them, and let them figure it out. Which is better management anyway.

Last month we had a partnership issue with another organization that would affect thousands of people. For us to fulfill our obligation, my department needed the other departments to chip in a *lot,* and the male director who reported to me was not getting that cooperation. I knew he was a smart, capable guy. So rather than solving it for him and telling him to go do X, Y, and Z, I encouraged him and involved him in the vision. I said, "You know what to do here. I'm sure you've dealt with people before who felt like they didn't own this deal and so they didn't deliver. Perhaps you might think about what would most excite them about your longer-term vision for the project, and go engage them in it."

That approach worked really well. You don't need to keep the vision only to yourself.

Insight 5: "I must be purposeful about balancing work and family"

I was struck that most of the highest-level women I interviewed had no children; there was a reason they had been able to devote extra time to career! One of the others, who has done well at prioritizing her family even as a leader in her field, told me, "You have to be aware of God's calling on your life. But that includes knowing when you are to *do* and when you are to step back."

> *"You have to be aware of God's calling on your life. But that includes knowing when to do and when to step back."*

Many women have found that stepping back from the workplace entirely for a time is the answer that allows them to prioritize their children while they are young. Others (like me) have tried to establish feasible work boundaries and stick with them regardless of the consequences, and/or have found the answer in trading off schedules with their husband, so the kids have a large amount of "dad time." Others have traded off the career track or jobs with the highest demands, pay, and prestige to gain a significantly reduced or flexible schedule. No answer is a one-size-fits-all. We must understand what will please God, make the hard decisions necessary to follow through, then be careful not to present God's answer for *us* as the right answer for everyone.

Not only have I personally wrestled with this issue, I've also created a video-driven study called *The Life Ready Woman* that helps us work through how to balance life as modern women from a biblical perspective (see www.LifeReady.com/woman for more information).

Insight 6: "Loving my neighbor instead of 'standing on my rights' will often accomplish more in the end"

The Christian women I interviewed found that the others-focused character that God asks of us will often bolster rather than undermine us in a challenging environment. In a competitive environment, it is easy to feel the need to "stand on your rights" ("I'm the leader, and I say we do it this way!"). But as Jesus demonstrated, and as research has found (such as in Jim Collins's book *Good to Great*), we can be servant leaders and accomplish much without compromising the authority entrusted to us.

The difficult cases, with difficult men, are often those where a different approach yields the most fruit. Louisa is the worship leader at her church and the wife of the pastor. She provided this example from when she was first asked to lead worship:

> The worship team was both men and women, and I really butted heads with the man on keyboards. He was older, a

difficult personality, and I could tell that he didn't like me leading worship. I was pretty intimidated by him, and I felt like I had to assert my authority or I would lose it.

Eventually, I was able to look deeper and realize that it wasn't about me. There was probably some deep insecurity on his part; he felt I did not respect all that he brought to the table. And you know what? Initially, I was intimidated enough that I didn't. But when I woke up to this, I saw all these talents I had brushed off. Once I realized that I needed to affirm him, he was a totally different guy.

Even though there was a way I wanted to do something, I would ask for his opinion. "From your perspective on keyboards, how do you think the transition ought to go?" And if it was a great idea, I would tell him so. Not only had I never asked before, I'd never given him that sort of feedback before.

That's honestly all I did. And although he's a hard person, he began to soften. We still didn't agree on everything, but his whole countenance seemed to soften, and worship was so much better.

Insight 7: "In an imperfect world, doing it right doesn't always guarantee that it will come out right"

Outside of heaven, injustice will always exist. We can do all we can to honor God and man in our relationships, and there is still no guarantee that it will come out right. As an accomplished operations executive named Bethany told me, "I've worked at more than my fair share of companies that were sexist, period. And I've learned that there are some times that you just can't change it, regardless of what you do."

When that happens, when there is true injustice, how should a woman of God respond? Lara gave a good perspective:

What it really comes down to is seeing this from an eternal perspective instead of an earthly one. The first thing to do when we experience injustice is to literally lay the injustice at God's feet. God says He is not only our advocate, but that vengeance belongs to Him. And Jesus is able to redeem sin, injustice, and false accusation. He is able to redeem those times we've been wounded or falsely accused. He's able to take something that is extremely toxic and high cost to us and is causing us to not bear the fruit we thought we should have, and He's able to redeem that. The Enemy would like us to believe that we are limited to the way things usually work in the world, but Jesus provides an override to the world's system. We have permission from God to ask for redemption!

Those three years where we weren't given the credit, where we weren't paid what we should have been, whatever the injustice—we have permission to ask for redemption for that. Just like God's promise to the Israelites that He will give back what the locusts have eaten.

But the second thing we must do is be willing to step back and look at the larger picture and realize that it's not about the next ten minutes, or even the next two years, but is actually positioned in terms of eternity. Sometimes God places us in a role so He can extend mercy over judgment. Sometimes we simply have to be willing to lay down our sense of right and justice. Yes, this was truly injustice, but ultimately how it gets resolved is up to God.

And trusting God for redemption does not rule out the possibility that you may to need make a change. As Bethany explained, "I don't think God means for His children to be abused. Sometimes your response will be to stay on, or find a different department or role. But sometimes the answer will be to know when you've done all you can do, the situation isn't going to change, and it is time to move on."

A LIFE THAT PLEASES HIM

Ultimately, we must recognize that God cares about and has plans for every aspect of our lives—including our work life and our work relationships with the men He has put in our path. He wants us to bring Him glory and honor wherever we are. And thankfully, God's presence and power are available to us to help us do just that.

As her final advice, Bethany issued this challenge, saying,

> In the end, our lives must be about furthering God's kingdom. And furthering the kingdom may mean putting ourselves on hold or taking the risk to look at things differently from the other person's point of view. It may mean walking across the room and treating someone differently because that is a higher calling. Whether it is men in the workplace or at home, we are called by God to support them and respect them and bring back the place of honor that I think we have lost in this country. In God's economy, this is not a zero-sum game. In treating others with respect, we gain respect for ourselves and the way God has created us as well.

Although Lara has attained worldly success, she echoed the theme of success in God's eyes:

> I would really like to see women shift their mind-set away from this apple of "personal success" the world is dangling

in front of us. Instead of, "How do I propel my career and achieve this success?" we should ask, "How do I enable the people around me to reach their potential in God?"

There's something to Eve having been created as a helpmeet. We as women do in fact tend to be more nurturing. In all environments, not just home, we need to ask: why are we wired that way, and how does God want to bring life through that wiring? What role is it that we're supposed to be playing in the market?

We have an incredible power and role we're supposed to fulfill in the business world. God never intended us to play second fiddle, but we are also supposed to allow His life to come through us instead of looking at people and trying to do it the world's way. There's incredible power in that.

> "We as women are more nurturing. We need to ask: why are we wired that way, and how does God want to bring life through that wiring?"

We've learned a lot about men in this journey together, and I hope each of you has begun to get a vision for how to apply your new knowledge. As we move forward, let's enjoy our new opportunities to take literally this exhortation in Romans from the apostle Paul: As far as it depends on you, live at peace with all men.

Acknowledgments

In a research project that spanned eight years, literally hundreds of people provided help, expertise, and insight along the way. While I cannot name them all here, some are acknowledged in earlier books, especially *For Women Only* and my novel *The Lights of Tenth Street*. All have my gratitude. That said, I must thank several critical groups of people on this project.

To the women and men who provided so much information and insight: The content of this book springs from the generosity of the men I interviewed and the dozens of people—men and women—who provided insight, helped set up meetings, networked me into their contacts, and generally made the research possible. Although I promised to keep them and their organizations anonymous, I am in their debt.

In addition to the research team named below, I want to thank the women who spent hours reading chapters, giving me feedback, and/or helping with specific aspects of the research, including Susan Conley, Alison Darrell, Sue Deagle, Carrie Delong, Paula Dumas, Wendy Shashoua, and Amy Smith. My thanks also to those who helped me conduct the "visual experiment," especially those at the InTouch studios in Atlanta and "Laurie Boss" for her time and talent. Special gratitude goes to Lisa Ryan who wielded the virtual microphone that started me on this road in the first place.

To the Research Team and others who work with me: At the front of the book are photographs of the core team that helped me conduct the research; design, test, and conduct the survey; analyze the results; and advise me on many aspects of content. This has been a massive team effort, and there would be no book without them.

To Chuck Cowan and Mauricio Vidaurre-Vega at Analytic Focus: As always, thanks for willingly pouring so many extra hours of effort and personal interest into this project. Chuck, each time we work together, I'm immensely thankful for your belief in what I'm doing and your willingness to bring your considerable expertise to bear on the survey-development process. To Felicia Rogers, Ramiro Davila, Scott Hanson, and the others at Decision Analyst: Over the years I have only grown more grateful for your outstanding work.

My heartfelt admiration and thanks go to my outstanding research analysts Jenny Reynolds and Jackie Feit Coleman, who braved everything from, respectively, the minutia of clinical neuroscience studies and detailed survey spreadsheets, to the prospect of being arrested while helping me test the survey (and nearly missing her graduate school graduation ceremony that night!). I'm grateful for other team members, such as Tally Whitehead, my column research assistant, whose great work in other areas allowed me to focus on the book.

To Calvin Edwards and Kim Rash: The massive amount of personal energy, time, interest, and insight each of you was willing to invest over the last seven years has made an incredible difference to the content and, hopefully, usefulness of the final book. I am almost embarrassed when I look back and tally up the hundreds of hours the two of your poured into the process. Thank you for your willing gift of time.

To Ann Browne: Thanks for bringing your personal and professional encouragement to bear over the years, and for being willing to step out of corporate America and partner with me in Human Factor Resources, to help readers go beyond the book in the corporate market.

And finally, most important, on my personal team I want to thank my director of operations, Linda Crews, for being so invested in this work and for her amazing way of keeping everything running; and my assistants over the years, Leslie Hettenbach, Karen Newby, Vance Hanifen, and Cathy Kidd, who cheerfully listened to and read through even the most difficult of interviews; categorized subjects and arranged meetings, itineraries, and focus groups until neither they nor I knew what city I was in anymore; and generally did an amazing job of keeping this messy author organized.

To both publishers: A book that is copublished between two different divisions has had many skilled minds involved, and they all have my thanks. I am especially grateful for my primary editors on this Christian edition: Dave Kopp at WaterBrook Multnomah, my editor on all my previous relationship books, whose structural help, words, and advice since 2003 have so thoroughly influenced my ability to put these books together. And Jeanette Thomason, whose work was so vital in turning the original Christian (Expanded) Edition of *The Male Factor* into this edition. My deep thanks also goes to Roger Scholl at Broadway Business, my original, primary editor on the general-market version of *The Male Factor*.

I'm also grateful for, among many others, Ken Petersen, Allison O'Hara, Lynettte Kittle at WaterBrook Multnomah, as well as the marketing and publicity team in New York. A special thanks also to Michael Palgon for his belief in and encouragement of this project.

And finally, a very special note to those who walked the road with me: I think only my personal staff and a few family and friends truly know how challenging and draining the last few years have been, and their support, help, prayer, and encouragement have been vital in allowing me to come through this with family, sanity, heart, and most brain cells intact.

I'm so thankful for the dozens of men and women who committed to personally supporting me in thought, word, and prayer. Thank you for such an important act of friendship.

I'm grateful for the love and encouragement of my parents and

Jeff's, Dick and Judy Reidinger, and Bill and Roberta Feldhahn. I'm especially grateful for two little squirts who have loved and encouraged their mother through a much longer process than this was intended to be.

To Jeff, my husband and best friend: Bud, there is no way I can ever thank you enough. I'm awed by your unfailing, unflinching love, advice, encouragement, and intensely practical help to all of us. I'm so grateful I turned left instead of right that day.

Ultimately, to the One who matters most: All of this is because of and dedicated to you.

Appendix

Emotions and the Male Brain

As you interact with men at work and at home, you have probably seen that men appear to handle emotion and interpersonal issues very differently than women. While certain aspects of this are based on personality, temperament, and personal choices, in large part it starts from the fact that the male brain simply handles emotion differently than the female brain. As noted in chapter 2, emotion can tend to fur up the gears in the male brain. Here are a few key reasons why.

EMOTION CAUSES A TRAFFIC JAM

Being able to assimilate, understand, and talk about emotion requires an enormous degree of multitasking communication between different parts of the brain, especially between the left and right hemispheres via the corpus callosum superhighway. That structure is 25 percent smaller in a man than in a woman, with much less of the connecting white matter that allows simultaneous processing of thoughts and other inputs, such as a surge of emotion.[1] By limiting the neural connections available, both factors make it difficult for a man to process a thought and a feeling at the same time. It also usually makes the process slower. By contrast, men's larger amount of gray matter within the corpus callosum makes their brains ideal to process information in a more deliberate, sequential and much deeper fashion.[2]

In a woman's brain, then, communication across hemispheres is a bit like an eight-lane superhighway. A woman has a lot of capacity to absorb and process an extra volume of traffic or input (such as thoughts and emotions). Traffic moves quickly, and since it takes a lot of traffic to clog things up, a woman can process a relatively high volume of emotion and think clearly at the same time. In a man, however, the infrastructure is more like a major parkway with multiple built-in traffic stops to allow for extra thinking time. With either type of infrastructure, all thoughts and emotions eventually will be processed, but a man's system usually isn't built to handle the same amount of volume as quickly. As a result, a surge of emotions can overwhelm a man's ability to think clearly, which is why men tend to instinctively shut down or set aside emotional traffic to deal with later.

While this infrastructure puts men at a disadvantage when trying to process many thoughts and emotions at once, its deliberate pace gives male brains the advantage of processing everything more deeply, so that nothing is missed due to neurological distractions, just as getting slowed down by rush-hour traffic gives you extra time to figure out the best way to handle that tricky nine a.m. meeting with your boss.

EMOTION TAPS NONTHINKING BRAIN REGIONS

When confronted with strong emotion, a man's brain, unlike a woman's, is predisposed to rely on an instinctive, nonthinking area. As Michael Gurian explains in his book *What Could He Be Thinking?*, "The male brain relies more heavily on brainstem activity than does the female brain, especially during emotive experience."[3] Translated, that means when a man is confronted with strong emotions in others or begins to experience them himself, his brain activity often reverts back to the brainstem, the more primitive, nonthinking brain region. The brainstem regulates automatic activities like digestion and is called the fight or flight center that we all revert to in a crisis. And according to a study by University of California psychologists, the male brain experiences strong emotions (like a crying woman) as a crisis—and thus jumps to that fight or flight center.[4]

This is another reason why the presence of emotion makes it difficult for a man to think clearly, and why men often feel a need to filter out emotion in order to think things through, make decisions, and get things done. (It is also one of the reasons why in relationships a woman can feel that a man goes into a fix-it mode when she's describing an emotional problem. She wants her feelings to be heard. He, on the other hand, instinctively recognizes that her feelings will impair his ability to help her deal with the problem, which is what he thinks she wants. So he automatically compartmentalizes to remove feelings from the equation.)

At work or home, when a man must deal with emotions directly, his adrenal system kicks his brain into a higher gear to handle the demands and anxiety of experiencing, thinking, and talking about those emotions and the reason for them. But as with any activity requiring an adrenaline surge, there's a weariness that occurs once it's over. That is probably why so many men describe emotions as exhausting.

In my interview with Cole, an executive search leader, most of his comments focused on this issue of men's perceptions of emotion. Cole was unusual for a man in having a high capacity to process emotions, yet at one point, discussing the large number of men who feel emotions are a waste of time, even he admitted,

> It's not just the time, the minutes. It's the energy. I am not
> a typical guy in some ways. I have high feminine scores for

qualities like empathy, but even for me, emotions take a lot of energy and there is only so much energy a person has during the day. For men there is nothing more draining than being in a spontaneous, unexpected emotional situation. A man's adrenaline has to kick into high gear to handle it. If it's a big emotional thing, we go from being very, very energized to being just exhausted when the adrenaline wears off. To a lesser degree, every single emotional encounter during the day creates a little of that exhaustion. It taps whatever energy resources we've got. And this is coming from a guy who tries to get other guys to realize that emotions can be a good thing.

NEURAL PATHS ARE MORE LIKELY TO BYPASS EMOTIONAL CENTERS

Women who feel themselves getting emotional may wonder how the men in the room are able to stay emotionally detached. Much of the reason has to do with an area in the middle brain called the cingulate gyrus, studied by a team of neuroscientists from the Brain-Body Institute in Ontario, Canada. As Michael Gurian describes it in layman's terms, "The cingulate gyrus is a very powerful emotion-processing element of the limbic system. The female brain processes more life experience through the cingulate gyrus than does the male. With more neural pathways to and from this gyrus in the female brain than in the male, the female brain is more emotion laden."[5]

In other words, one reason men don't experience as much emotion isn't just because they compartmentalize it out, but because their brain signals often bypass the emotional centers that would have added on emotion in the first place.[6]

As noted in chapter 2, men simply feel a bit less equipped to handle emotional and interpersonal issues. Research published in the professional journal *NeuroImage* shows this is because men's brains have far less oxytocin, the tend-and-befriend hormone that allows people to recognize and empathize with one another.[7] Also, neurobiologists at the University of California found that the male brain's structural focus on its action center, the amygdala, makes it less likely to pick up subtle signals of emotion in the first place.[8] Certainly, men pick up those signals at some point, but usually at a higher level of intensity than the point at which women would first notice them.

Men and women are both created the way they are for a reason, with different purposes and strengths. It is helpful to be aware of these factors, so we can appreciate and work with the purposes behind the male and female brain wiring, rather than getting frustrated that each of us is not like the other.

Discussion Questions

This guide is designed to be flexible, so you can pick and choose the questions and topics most relevant to you, your group, and your workplace. You may want to keep a notebook handy to record any actionable insights. If your group chooses to do one or more of the Application Actions, remember to allow time during your next group session for reporting on how it went.

1. "It's Not Personal; It's Business"

1. What points do you view as most important in this chapter, for you? Why?
2. Provide an example of a time in which you may have been viewed as breaking one of men's "natural laws" of Work World. How did that affect how you were perceived in the short and long term? What might you have done differently to change that perception?
3. Provide an example of a time when you believe you were viewed by male colleagues as "doing it right" in this area (i.e., avoiding bringing Personal World rules into Work World). What specifically was it that was perceived well (tone of voice, word choice in a meeting…)?
4. What can women do to advance alternative viewpoints (for example, not such a rigid distinction between Personal versus Work World) without undermining how they are perceived?
5. Identify the ways in which there is value in compartmentalizing between Personal World and Work World. Identify the ways in which such compartmentalization is detrimental.

6. How can you become a custodian of your position, as men said is a Work World rule? How do you summon passion about your job and at the same time detach enough so as to not take things personally in that position?

7. Did it surprise you to hear how deeply men feel affected by emotional pain? Why or why not? How does this make you feel toward male co-workers? (Frustrated? More compassionate...?)

8. How might you consider a colleague's feelings when implementing a business decision without that being seen as allowing feelings to affect the decision itself? Have you seen this done or experienced it? With what effects?

APPLICATION ACTIONS

• In the short term (this week, or until your group meets again), observe examples of women or men who seem to be bringing their Personal World into Work World. Record how that is perceived by others.

• Observe and record your own patterns and interactions that illustrate veering from the "natural laws" of Work World. If possible, experiment with a completely different approach to one or more of these situations and record the results.

2. "She's Crying—What Do I Do?"

1. What points do you view as most important in this chapter, for you? Why?

2. Hasn't every woman felt emotional at work one time or another? Tell about a time this happened, how you handled it, and how it was perceived. Now that you've had

some distance from that situation, how might you have handled it differently?

3. Once a woman suspects that she's viewed as not thinking clearly, what strategies might demonstrate that she is?

4. What's worked for you in the past in taming a rising anger or impulse to cry?

5. Biologically, a woman's brain function tends to add emotion, and women often find it natural (and valuable) to process verbally. Since both could be viewed inaccurately by men, how can women develop an "edit function" around how we express emotion? In particular, how can we do it in a way that is viewed as actually adding value to a given situation?

6. Looking at the list of things that men see as "getting emotional," other than crying, what situations and people are most likely to trigger that behavior for you? Frustration at being sidelined? Someone not "getting" what you are trying to explain? Being criticized? Does identifying the triggers help you prepare to manage the situation differently?

7. When have you felt or experienced emotion at work as a strength?

8. How can women help male colleagues understand the value and capacity of female emotional wiring?

APPLICATION ACTIONS

- Keep an eye out for any situation around you in which men may view someone as "getting emotional." Observe what happens, how the relevant person is perceived, and, most important, what specific factors could have changed that perception, if necessary.

- If there is an occasion in which you realize you may be perceived as becoming emotional, put into practice one or more of the tips you have identified to counter that perception, and record what happens.

3. "If I Let Down My Guard, the World Will Stop Spinning"

1. What points do you view as most important in this chapter, for you? Why?
2. Do you, as a woman, ever feel the "world might stop spinning" pressure in any type of situation? If so, does that help you understand and relate to the male views in this chapter?
3. When have you felt like your male colleagues thought you were "all in" with the team? When have you suspected they didn't feel that way? What was it that you did that led to each perception?
4. What are some specific words and actions that might signal to others that you and other female colleagues are "all in" and sharing the weight of the world? Which might you be able to adopt in your workplace?
5. Men might agree that, technically, it shouldn't matter when you leave the office if you get your work done, but emotionally, it often signals that the person isn't sharing the team's pain. Which factor is more important: your schedule and family needs, or their perception? What can you do to manage how you are perceived, if you choose to prioritize your need to leave the office at a certain time?
6. In your workplace, do you ever see either women or men seeming to value relationship more than results? As a woman, how do you think relationship contributes to results in business? What might men miss about this?

APPLICATION ACTIONS

- If possible, identify one or more examples of someone who is perceived as achieving results but not as being "all in" with the team. Record what it is, specifically, that is leading to that perception. Next, find an example of someone who people clearly think is "all in," and record what leads to that perception. Capture any valuable strategies that come to light.
- Experiment with one or more strategies that signal you are "all in" and sharing the weight of the world. (In particular, find a way to signal this to someone who may believe that you aren't, if applicable.) Record what happens both over the short term and the long term.

4. "I Can't Handle It"

1. What points do you view as most important in this chapter, for you? Why?
2. Which of the "little things" men cited as frustrating do you most tend to fall into, if any? Give an example, and share what specifically it was about your words and actions (or men's perceptions) that led to that irritation.
3. If you are the type to provide details as you explain something, how do you know the appropriate amount of detail and what is "too much"? What specifically can you do to edit yourself in communicating information you deliver in person or in e-mails?
4. If you realize you have a tendency to "overreact," how can you stop yourself?
5. If you sometimes have difficulty "letting it go," why is that the case, and what can you do to approach such a situation differently?

6. What are some of the other "little things" you've seen frustrating men at work?

7. Can you identify any common patterns in situations, environments, or people that would tell you when to be most aware of the likelihood of irritation, and the need to avoid it? For example: "When the project is down to the wire and my boss disagrees with me, I tend to keep pushing." Or, "Because I know so much about the numbers, when I present a financial analysis, I go into too much detail on the background of each figure."

8. Are there situations in which irritating others is necessary for professional effectiveness? If so, how should you navigate them to be a benefit instead of a detriment?

APPLICATION ACTION

- If there is an occasion in which you realize you might be close to tripping the "irritation wire" (or have already done so), put into practice one or more of the strategies from this discussion time, and record what happens.

5. "Suck It Up"

1. What points do you view as most important in this chapter, for you? Why?

2. Provide one or two examples of a situation you have observed where someone may be viewed as not "sucking it up." (By, for example, not pushing through obstacles, talking about how hard one is working, asking for help, or asking for "different standards" in schedule, projects, or flexibility.) If these situations are viewed negatively, specifically what contributes to that? Conversely, if these situations continue to be viewed positively and don't result in a negative perception, why is that?

3. In situations that you have seen where someone is indeed viewed negatively for not "sucking it up," what might that person have done differently to improve how she was perceived, even if her choices (such as schedule flexibility) remained the same?

4. How do you feel about the notion that no one can have it all, at the same time? Does this advice seem reasonable and realistic or make you frustrated or angry? Tell about some women you've seen who seem to have both a demanding home life raising children and a leadership position at work. How do they seem to make it work? List all possible trade-offs (for the women and others) that could be happening to make that possible (for example, "She only gets six hours of sleep each night" or "Her husband only works a part-time schedule in order to take on childcare duties" or "Her kids can't do sports since she isn't home in time to drive them," etc.).

5. When men say it's important to signal your day-to-day commitment, what ideas of how to do that come to mind for you? What does commitment look like in your work-place, and how can you show it even beyond the important factor of availability?

6. Men believe that figuring out things on your own equates to confidence and capability. Has asking for help ever hurt you at work—possibly without you realizing it at the time? When has it benefited you or a project? How can you request help (or offer it) without planting doubts in your male colleagues' minds about your ability (or theirs) to solve a problem?

7. Do you think it is fair that negotiating a different or more flexible schedule can be viewed as "special treat-ment"? Have you or someone you know negotiated such a schedule, and if so, what was the impact on both

perceptions and the work itself? Is there anything further you can do to improve how you or the situation is perceived?

APPLICATION ACTIONS

- Observe those around you to identify as many situations as possible where someone is viewed as *not* "sucking it up." Record specifically what they did and what they might have done differently to improve others' perceptions even if certain choices (such as schedule flexibility) remained the same.
- If you have a flexible schedule, what might you do that you are not already doing (if anything) to improve how that is perceived? Implement one or more short-term ideas, and record the results.

6. "I'm Not as Confident as I Look"

1. What points do you view as most important in this chapter, for you? Why?
2. About men's hidden self-doubt: Describe a time you believe you've seen evidence that a man was fearing failure on the job or feeling a bit insecure. Did you recognize this for what it was at the time? How can you recognize it in the future?
3. Because of their private self-doubt, some men may receive some of what you say and do as a signal of disrespect or that you don't trust their judgment. Have you ever experienced this? What specifically might you change in order to improve how your words or actions are received?
4. Specifically, asking, "Why?" can often be misunderstood. List alternative ways of saying the same thing that won't send the (unintentional) message that your colleague doesn't know what he is doing.

5. If you've ever bruised a male ego at work, what have you done about it going forward? How have you healed your working relationship? What worked? What didn't? What might you try next time?

6. In a scenario where, in your experience and knowledge, you strongly disagree with your male colleagues or boss, how can you express your concerns without sending a damaging disrespect signal and yet accomplish your business goals?

APPLICATION ACTION

- Look for opportunities to experiment with different approaches to a male boss or colleague that will signal respect instead of risking unintentional disrespect. Record specifically what you said and/or did, and what the response was.

7. "That Low-Cut Blouse Undercuts Her Career"

1. What points do you view as most important in this chapter, for you or (if applicable) for those you manage or mentor? Why?

2. Do you think this issue might impact you—that you sometimes wear outfits men might perceive as sexual and distracting? If so, how do you feel about what the men said in this chapter? (Irritated? Convicted? Offended? Desiring to change immediately?) Similarly, what are the reasons why you might sometimes dress that way, and what do you think about whether you should reevaluate those outfits?

3. If this issue does not apply to you but does apply to women you manage, work with, or mentor, how can you address this awkward issue with them most effectively? Should you?

4. In the control group of women on the survey, most of those that dressed to emphasize their figure said they weren't intending to cause a sexual distraction for men; they wanted to feel confident and/or wear what was in style. What is the compulsion behind this female desire? (Is it simply a desire to feel attractive? To receive affirmation? What else?) Does understanding what is behind this desire provide any assistance at all with how to address this issue in the workplace?

5. Most workplaces, blue and white collar, have casual dress days, where employees are allowed to wear more relaxed and comfortable clothing. Are there times in which taking advantage of casual days might be technically allowable but still unwise?

APPLICATION ACTIONS

• Ask a man you are personally close to (husband, boyfriend, brother) for a tutorial on exactly what feminine clothes will trigger the sexual response and distraction in men. Ask this man that you trust to spend fifteen minutes with you in a public place where there will be many people walking by in everyday attire (not evening dress, and not with coats on); have him tell you each time a woman walks by wearing something that would cause difficulty concentrating, if it was seen in the workplace. Record what you learn.

• Get a reality check about your own attire. Ask the man you are personally close to whether you ever wear any clothes that would cause that distraction factor in the workplace. Ask for specifics (which outfits, if he can remember), and assure him that you want him to be honest.

8. "The Most Important Thing"

1. What points do you view as most important in this chapter, for you? Why?
2. In the research for this book, many men stated their appreciation for what women brought to the workplace. What positive things have you heard men say about female colleagues in your business? Does this lend itself to any ideas for areas you might emphasize for yourself?
3. Think about a woman at work that you see as a role model. What feminine qualities did she display, and how did they impact her effectiveness at work? What can you take from her example for how you speak and act in your workplace?
4. In what ways can you be genuine and authentic at work, while still being perceived as speaking the language of the male culture?
5. Do you believe there might be a downside to being genuine and authentic in the workplace? What strategies might allow you to be yourself without triggering the downside?
6. When have you seen a woman try to act like a man in order to get ahead at work? What does that look like? What effect did she have on those around her?
7. In an effort to relate more often or better with male colleagues, have you done something "like the guys," so to speak? For instance, have you gone golfing with men at work just to connect and when you wouldn't do so ordinarily? What happened? How did things go, and did you notice any effect in your relationships? Would you do that again, and why or why not?
8. What can men and women build together in your workplace that men alone or women alone could not? Talk about the qualities women and men each bring to the job that gets business done and moving forward.

APPLICATION ACTION

- Observe one or more people around you who seem to be living up to the men's "most important advice" to "be yourself, be competent, and you'll do well." Observe what specifically they do that results in being viewed positively. Record any observations that might help you going forward.

9. Putting It in Perspective

1. What points do you view as most important in this chapter, for you? Why?
2. One woman advised that when we are baffled by male colleagues, we can ask God how to handle them. Have you ever given over to God a particular tension or difficult relationship with a male colleague? How did you do so, and what happened?
3. Do you have any current baffling or frustrating situations with a male colleague? What might you pray for going forward? Does the context of this book provide any suggestions or answers for how to proceed?
4. How might it change your interaction with male colleagues if you think of God as your real boss, as if you were working for God and not for people?
5. Think about your interactions with male colleagues in the recent past (e.g., the last week, the last three months, etc.). How have they seen Christ in you? Describe a defining moment of this, if there is one, and how you might create more of those moments.
6. How do you balance work and family in a way that allows you to prioritize what is most important, but is still perceived well? Who have you seen do this well? What

worked for them? Have you seen men in your workplace do this? What works for them?

APPLICATION ACTION

- Pick one thing you want to change based on all you've learned in this book and in this discussion group. Put it into practice and record what you observe as a result, over time. (You might want to share the results, either formally or informally, with others in your group going forward, and continue to encourage one another.)

Notes

Chapter 1: "It's Not Personal; It's Business"

1. The cross-tabbed, tallied answer represents all men who
actually did or didn't expect different behavior in the
workplace, based on their answer(s) to several later questions. The tallied answer is comprised of those who gave one
or more of the following answers on the survey (as seen at
ForWomenOnlyWorkplace.com): (1) on Q1 (the original
question noted here); (1) on Q2; (1) or (2) on Q4; (1) on
Q18.1, Q18.2, or Q18.5; (2) on Q18.7; (1) on Q23 or Q23.
This tallied answer isn't a perfect comparison, since the
questions were not able to compare a man's response to a
"personal" situation at work to that of a similar situation in
his personal life. However, those answer choices would
commonly be the opposite of those considered appropriate
in a personal setting (such as not considering another
person's feelings when making a decision that affected
them). Thus, while the comparison isn't perfect, the tallied
answer is likely to be a somewhat more realistic representa-
tion of how a man actually feels about whether the work and
personal worlds function differently.
2. Ruben C. Gur, Bruce I. Turetsky, Mie Matsui, Michelle Yan,
Warren Bilker, Paul Hughett, and Raquel E. Gur, "Sex
Differences in Brain Gray and White Matter in Healthy
Young Adults: Correlations with Cognitive Performance,"
Journal of Neuroscience 19, no. 10 (May 15, 1999): 4065–72.
3. Rita Carter, *Mapping the Mind* (Berkeley: University of
California Press, 1998).

4. Reuven Achiron and Anat Achiron, "Development of the Human Fetal Corpus Callosum: A High-Resolution, Cross-Sectional Sonographic Study," *Ultrasound in Obstetrics and Gynecology* 18, no. 4 (October 2001): 343–47.
5. Gur et al., "Sex Differences in Brain Gray and White Matter," 4065–72.

Chapter 3: "If I Let Down My Guard, the World Will Stop Spinning"

1. The full question listed eight actual quotes separately (discussed both in this chapter and chapter 6) and asked the survey takers to separately evaluate each of them, as follows: "Below are several quotes from various successful business-men about how they privately feel at times. Do you sometimes find yourself instinctively feeling this way? (When answering, please consider how you actually feel, regardless of whether you think it is logical, or whether you 'should' feel that way.)" Answer choices were "I feel like this regularly," "I feel like this sometimes," and "I rarely or never feel like this." Responses to this particular question: 1) I feel like this regularly, 28 percent; 2) I feel like this sometimes, 52 percent; 3). I rarely or never feel like this, 20 percent.
2. Dictionary.com, s.v. "entropy," http://dictionary.reference .com/browse/entropy.

Chapter 4: "I Can't Handle It"

1. Barbara and Allan Pease, *Why Men Don't Listen and Women Can't Read Maps* (New York: Broadway Books, 1998), 90.
2. Jeffery Tobias Halter, "Influencing Men, Influencing Women: Gender Strategies for Achieving Results" (talk, Atlanta, GA, February 5, 2009). Used by permission.

Chapter 5: "Suck It Up"

1. Jeff Chu, "10 Questions for Meredith Vieira," *Time*, August 27, 2006, www.time.com/time/magazine/article/0,9171,137 6220,00.html.
2. U.S. Department of Labor, Bureau of Labor Statistics, "Highlights of Women's Earnings in 2000," Report 952, August 2001, www.bls.gov/cps/cpswom2000.pdf.
3. See Denise Venable, "The Wage Gap Myth," National Center for Policy Analysis, April 12, 2002, www.ncpa.org/pub/ba392. Also see Judy Goldberg Dey and Catherine Hill, "Behind the Pay Gap," American Association of University Women, April 2007, www.aauw.org/learn/research/upload/behindPayGap.pdf.

Chapter 6: "I'm Not as Confident as I Look"

1. See chap. 3, n. 1 for further explanation on the format of this survey question.
2. See chap. 3, n. 1 for further explanation on the format of this survey question.
3. The question was: "In which of the following areas, if any, do you sometimes feel less than confident, or question how others view you?" Of the men surveyed, 74 percent chose one or more of the different insecurities listed, while 26 percent chose "None of the above; I rarely struggle with confidence in any of these areas."

Chapter 7: "That Low-Cut Blouse Undercuts Her Career"

1. Because there is no standard definition of what constitutes "being visual," there is no way to give a precise number for what percentage of women are visual. However, although

estimates from different sources vary widely (from roughly 5 to 25 percent), the upper ranges appear to cluster around 20 to 25 percent—and since Michael Gurian estimates that roughly 25 percent of people have what he calls "bridge brains" (brains that are true to their gender, but also have some wiring similar to that of the opposite sex), that figure seems to be a safe upper estimate.

2. Tim Koscik, Dan O'Leary, David J. Moser, Nancy C. Andreasen, and Peg Nopoulos, "Sex Differences in Parietal Lobe Morphology: Relationship to Mental Rotation Performance," *Brain and Cognition* 69, no. 3 (April 2009): 451–59.

3. L. Kilpatrick, D. H. Zald, J. V. Pardo, and L. Cahill, "Sex-Related Differences in Amygdala Functional Connectivity During Resting Conditions." *NeuroImage* 30, no. 2 (April 2006): 452–61.

4. Michael Gurian, *What Could He Be Thinking?* (New York: St. Martin's, 2003), 107–9.

5. Itzhak Aharon, Nancy Etcoff, Dan Ariely, Christopher F. Chabris, Ethan O'Connor, and Hans C. Breiter, "Beautiful Faces Have Variable Reward Value: fMRI and Behavioral Evidence," *Neuron* 32, no. 3 (November 2001): 537–51.

6. John Stossel, "The Ugly Truth About Beauty: Like It or Not, Looks Do Matter," August 23, 2002, http://abcnews .go.com/2020/story?id=123853.

7. David M. Buss, *The Evolution of Desire* (New York: Basic Books, 1994), 71.

8. Stephan Hamann, Rebecca A. Herman, Carla L. Nolan, and Kim Wallen, "Men and Women Differ in Amygdala Response to Visual Sexual Stimuli," *Nature Neuroscience* 7, no. 4 (April 2004): 411–16.

9. Richard Restak, *The Brain* (New York: Bantam, 1984), 197.

10. Walt Larimore and Barb Larimore, *His Brain, Her Brain* (Grand Rapids: Zondervan, 2008), 46–47.
11. Joseph LeDoux, "Emotional Memory Systems in the Brain," *Behavioral Brain Research* 58, nos. 1–2 (December 1993), 69–79; "Emotion, Memory, and the Brain," *Scientific American*, June 1994, 50–57; "Emotion and the Limbic System Concept." *Concepts in Neuroscience.*

Chapter 8: "The Most Important Thing"

1. The comments of the other respondents were split among a dozen other types of substantive advice—in particular the suggestions that women be cautious about how they dress and about how they display emotions. (You can see a broad sampling of the men's word-for-word answers at www.For WomenOnlyWorkplace.com.) Of the 602 male survey takers, several men did not provide a substantive answer to the question, and several others provided advice in more than one area. The total number of substantive comments was 581.
2. Several of the survey takers' quotes included in this chapter are edited for length, grammar, or clarity.

Chapter 9: Putting It in Perspective

1. There is an ongoing debate over the specific, limited question of church governance, but that is beyond the scope of this book.

Appendix: Emotions and the Male Brain

1. Reuven Achiron and Anat Achiron, "Development of the Human Fetal Corpus Callosum: A High-Resolution,

Cross-Sectional Sonographic Study," *Ultrasound in Obstetrics and Gynecology* 18, no. 4 (October 2001): 343–47.

2. Ruben C. Gur, Bruce I. Turetsky, Mie Matsui, Michelle Yan, Warren Bilker, Paul Hughett, and Raquel E. Gur, "Sex Differences in Brain Gray and White Matter in Healthy Young Adults: Correlations with Cognitive Performance," *Journal of Neuroscience* 19, no. 10 (May 15, 1999): 4065–72.

3. Michael Gurian, *What Could He Be Thinking?* (New York: St. Martin's, 2003), 83.

4. Shelley E. Taylor, Laura Cousino Klein, Brian P. Lewis, Tara L. Gruenewald, Regan A. R. Gurung, and John A. Updegraff, "Biobehavioral Responses to Stress in Females: Tend-and-Befriend, Not Fight-or-Flight," *Psychological Review* 107, no. 3 (July 2000): 411–29.

5. Gurian, *What Could He Be Thinking?* 84.

6. Geoffrey B. C. Hall, Sandra F. Witelson, Henry Szechtman, and Claude Nahmias, "Sex Differences in Functional Activation Patterns Revealed by Increased Emotion Processing Demands," *NeuroReport* 15, no. 2 (February 9, 2004): 219–23.

7. Zenab Amin, C. Neill Epperson, R. Todd Constable, and Turhan Canli, "Effects of Estrogen Variation on Neural Correlates of Emotional Response Inhibition," *NeuroImage* 32, no. 1 (August 2006): 457–64.

8. Larry Cahill and Anda van Stegeren, "Sex-Related Impairment of Memory for Emotional Events with -Adrenergic Blockade," *Neurobiology of Learning and Memory* 79, no. 1 (January 2003): 81–88.

Go Beyond the Book

If you want to learn more, or move from information to application, this is where you start!

ForWomenOnlyWorkplace.com

Find essential tools for personal development, peer coaching, mentoring, management or training; exchange ideas and solutions with other women in the workplace.

FIND:

- Workbook, including case studies and questions for individual and group application
- Extra chapter not included in the book
- Community forums with others who have great ideas for life application
- Complete survey results, including verbatim answers to the final questions
- Research not included in the book
- Input from experts
- Links for training and speaking options

Come share your stories and what has worked for you, hear from others, and continue the journey!

ForWomenOnlyWorkplace.com

The ONLY Series

More Than 1.5 Million Copies Sold

Best-selling authors Shaunti & Jeff Feldhahn and Lisa & Eric Rice draw on groundbreaking national surveys and thousands of personal interviews to offer life-changing, eye-opening truths about all the people you care about most—truths that have now transformed millions of relationships.

For Women Only

What is he really thinking?

A thoroughly researched, yet easy to read book on the inner lives of men and what they are really thinking and feeling.

Discussion guide available separately.

For Men Only

A straightforward guide to the inner lives of women

Unlock the mysterious ways of women, and discover what you can do today to improve your relationship.

Discussion guide available separately.

For Parents Only

For every bewildered parent there's a kid longing to be understood

Insight from extensive research that addresses the things parents often don't "get" about their kids.

Discussion guide available separately.

For Young Women Only

Unlock the Mystery of Guy-World

Dive into the mysterious inner-workings of the teen-age male mind and begin to understand why guys say and do what they do.

Discussion journal available separately.

For Young Men Only

A Guys Guide to the Alien Gender

Find out the real truth about what teenage girls think, what they want, and how average teen guys can build healthy friendships with girls.

Study guide included.

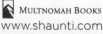 MULTNOMAH BOOKS
www.shaunti.com